THE WISDOM OF W

A collection of proverbs

By Paul Barrett · Photographs by Charles and Patricia Aithie

Published by UWIC Press, UWIC, Cardiff CF23 6XD
e-mail: najones@uwic.co.uk
ISBN 1-902724-29-1

Picture editor & production: Cathy Grove
Design: Andy Dark
Scanning: Caple Miller
Printing: Traxdata Wales Ltd.

This book has been typeset using the fonts, Palatino and Frutiger and has printed on Celestial Gloss 300gsm and 150gsm.

Paul Barrett was born in Abersychan, South Wales, where his family links with coal mining go back generations. After Monmouth School he studied and worked in England, Spain, France and Sweden. Previously Marketing Manager for the Wales Tourist Board, he is currently manager of the Enterprise Centre at the Welsh School of Hospitality, Tourism & Leisure at UWIC. He has written for television, national magazines and newspapers and speaks seven European languages.

Charles Aithie worked for ten years as a geologist before becoming a photographer, specialising in landscapes. **Patricia Aithie** studied Fine Art, before travelling and living in the Middle and Far East with Charles for five years. They returned to Wales to set up *ffotograff*, a photolibrary and agency specialising in travel, exploration and the arts, and now supply book publishers, magazines and newspapers. They are also well known for their postcards of Wales and are frequently commissioned to work on book projects.

FOREWORD

Visiting a country without understanding its culture is like watching a rugby match without comprehending the rules – both bewildering and unfulfilling. We trust that this book will give you a brief insight into the culture of Wales, one of the oldest in Europe, by looking at our society through our proverbs and through the unique images that accompany them.

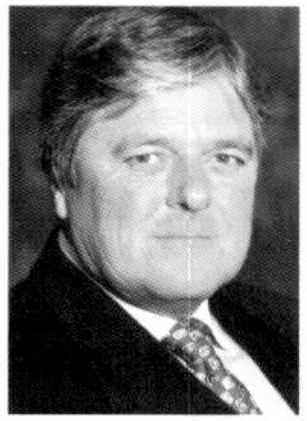

This book is compiled by Paul Barrett, author and specialist in Welsh culture, and Pat and Charles Aithie, who have taken some of the most memorable pictures of Wales. I am sure that 'The Wisdom of Wales' celebrates the uniqueness of our country and also provides fresh insights for those who wish to revisit the experience of Wales.

We don't always need signposts to find a special place. This book has no signposts either, but it will take you to many places that are timeless and very special.

Croeso i Gymru. Welcome to Wales.

Phillip Evans. CHAIRMAN WALES TOURIST BOARD

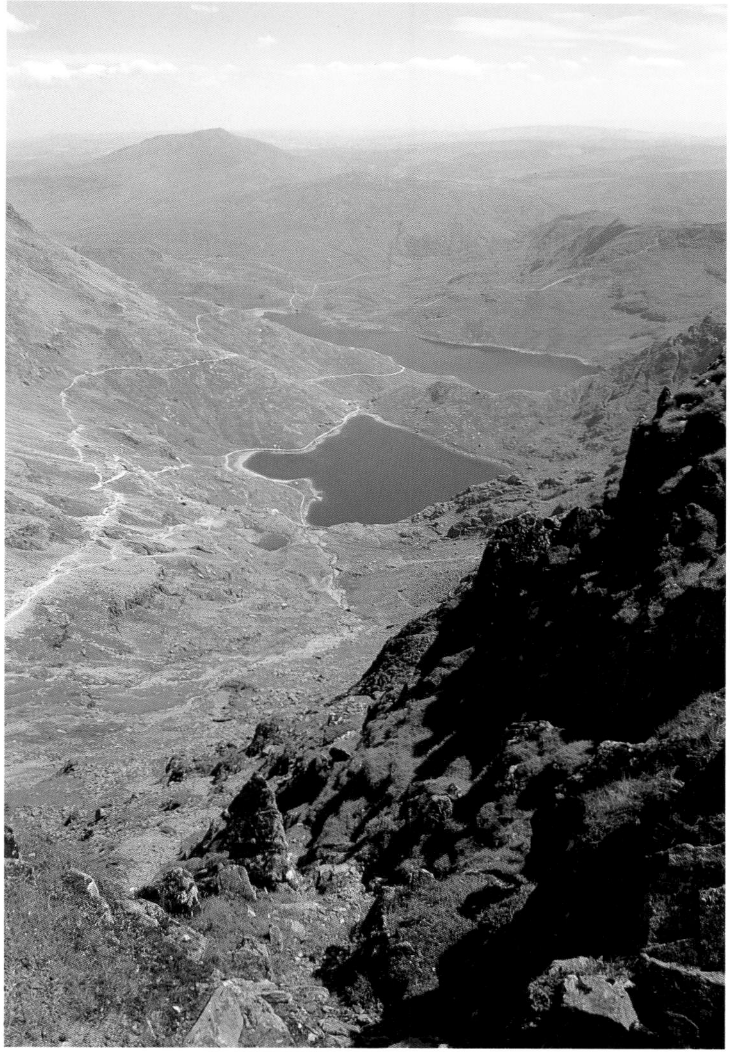

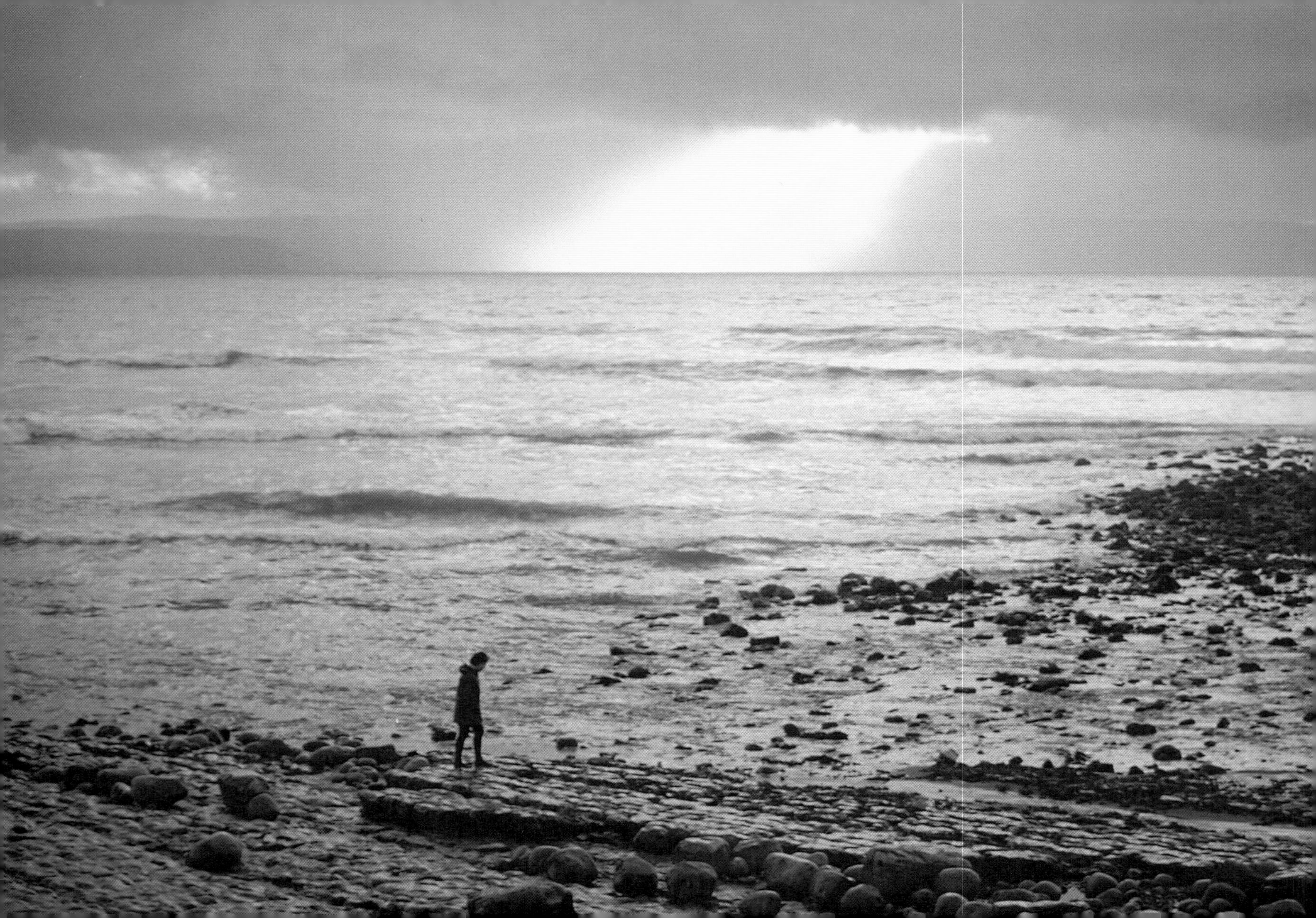

INTRODUCTION

Plant gwirionedd yw hen ddiarhebion
Old proverbs are the children of truth

*T*oday, on a universal scale, the Welsh language may seem something of an irrelevance. After all, those of us who have a good knowledge of the language are only a small pocket of about a million people, on the Atlantic edge of Europe, scudding about in the eddies of another language so powerful that the world has never seen its like.

So where does that leave Welsh? Isn't it an anachronism, in a world of increasing homogeneity, where we are all poised to race down the information superhighway?

Similar thoughts were raised in the nineteenth century, when the government of the time took draconian steps to stamp out the Welsh language 'for our own good'. But somehow, despite this - and despite one of the greatest population influxes within a given time and area that the world has ever seen - the Welsh language and culture are still surviving; education through the medium of Welsh is increasing at a tremendous rate due to demand from the grass roots.

Two thousand years before the advent of languages like English, French and German, the forerunner to Modern Welsh was spoken throughout Europe by the Celtic tribes that inhabited it, from the Bosphorus in the east, to the Atlantic in the west. The Celts believed that wisdom and learning should be committed to memory and transmitted orally: the use of proverbs was probably one way of doing this.

Thus, in some small way, this collection of proverbs brings us the distilled wisdom of many peoples and several millennia. Reading through them you will find yourself entering a world that is quite different from the one we inhabit today. But I hope it is one that you will still find relevant.

The photographs of Pat and Charles Aithie reflect the Wales of today, as well as our inheritance. They add a dimension to the proverbs that is at times poignant, at times humorous and, at others, timeless. I am aware how fortunate I am to have worked with them on this.

Cenedl heb iaith cenedl heb galon
A nation without a language has no heart

PAUL BARRETT

Y TYWYDD / THE WEATHER

When we were more self-sufficient, growing our own food and living in houses that were by no means as comfortable or healthy as they are today, the weather was extremely important: if the expected conditions did not occur when they were supposed to, it could mean death.

One of the first pieces of advice is that 'The best thing to do with regard to the weather is to keep quiet about it' - which is probably sound advice anywhere in Britain. However, not only would this cut our greetings and conversations rather short, but we would also be compelled to ignore a large number of Welsh proverbs!

Niwl y gwanwyn gwasarn gwynt
Niwl yr haf gwasarn tes
Niwl y cynhaeaf gwasarn glaw
Niwl y gaeaf gwasarn eira

Spring mist the harbinger of wind
Summer mist the harbinger of heat
Autumn mist the harbinger of rain
Winter mist the harbinger of snow

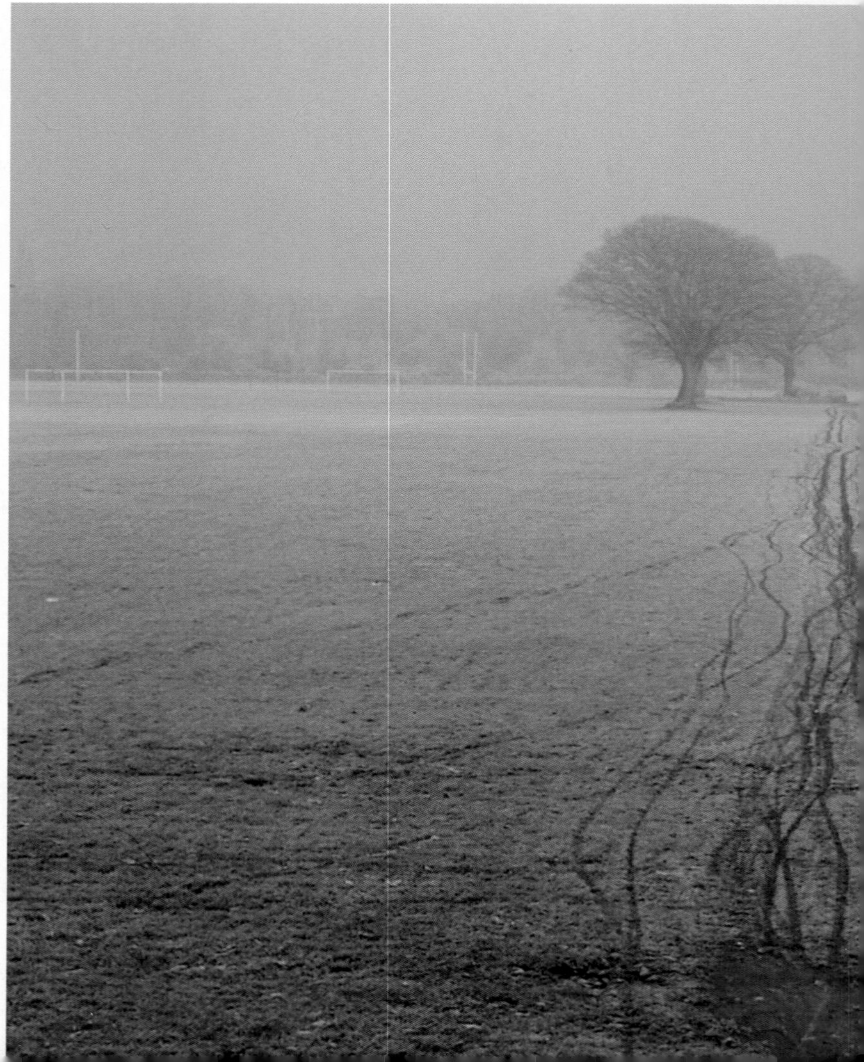

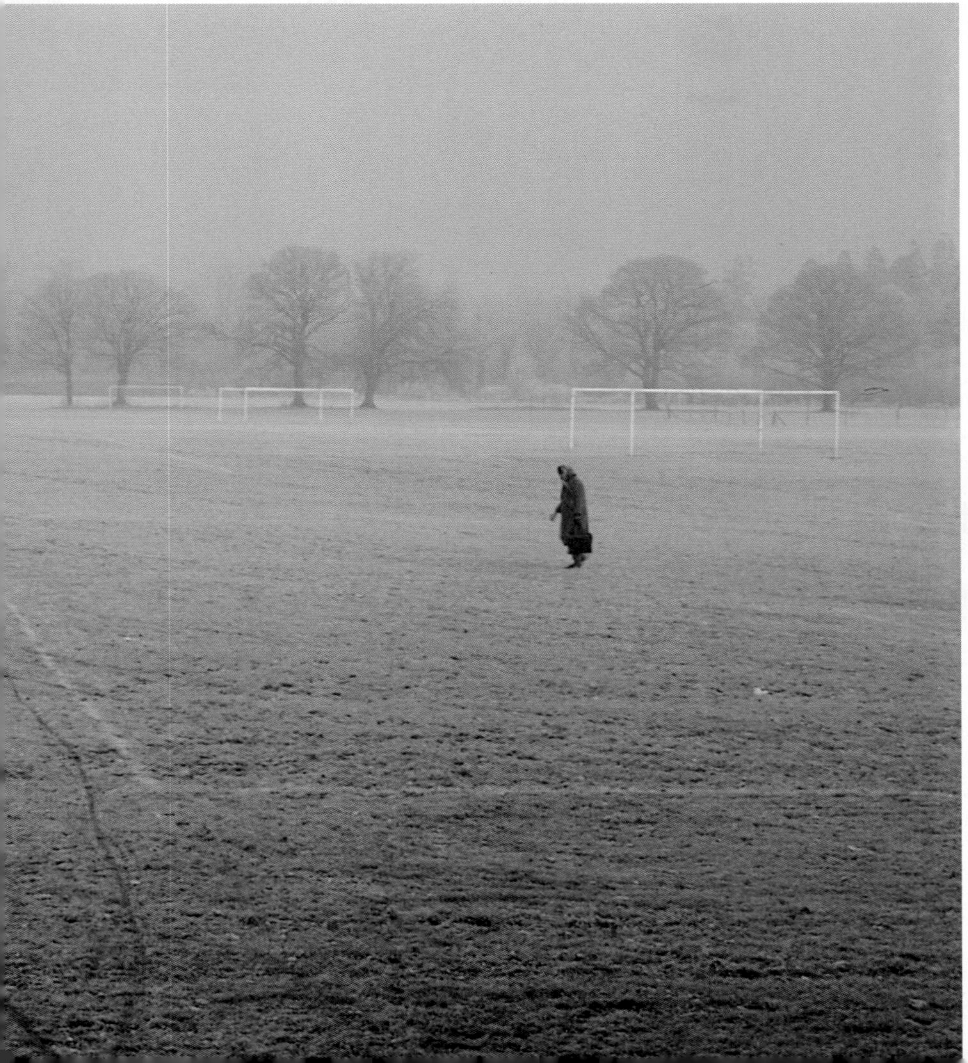

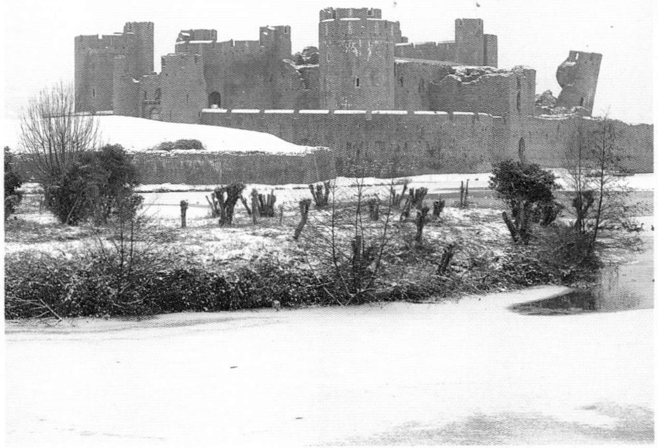

The snake has not always been a reptile that is disliked. The Romans, Greeks and Celts linked it with fertility, even the guardian of treasure. Giraldus Cambrensis told a story of a Pembrokeshire well in which there lay a torc, guarded by two snakes that bit would-be thieves. But later times have shown only a distaste for snakes, as this proverb underlines.

Chwefror chwyth y neidr o'i nyth
February will blow the snake out of his nest

Haul yn Ionawr ni mad welawr, Mawrth a Chwefror a'i dialawr
March and February will avenge January sunshine

It is clear that the end of the winter could finish off people and animals. In more northerly climates it is such a depressing time that this is the most common period, even today, for people to commit suicide.

Os daw Mawrth i mewn fel oen, â allan fel llew
If March comes in like a lamb, it will go out like a lion

Mawrth a ladd, Ebrill a fling
March will kill, April will flay

Ni saif eira yn Ebrill mwy nag wŷ ar ben ebill
April snow stays no longer than an egg on the top of a gimlet

Ebrill garw, porchell marw
A rough April, dead piglets

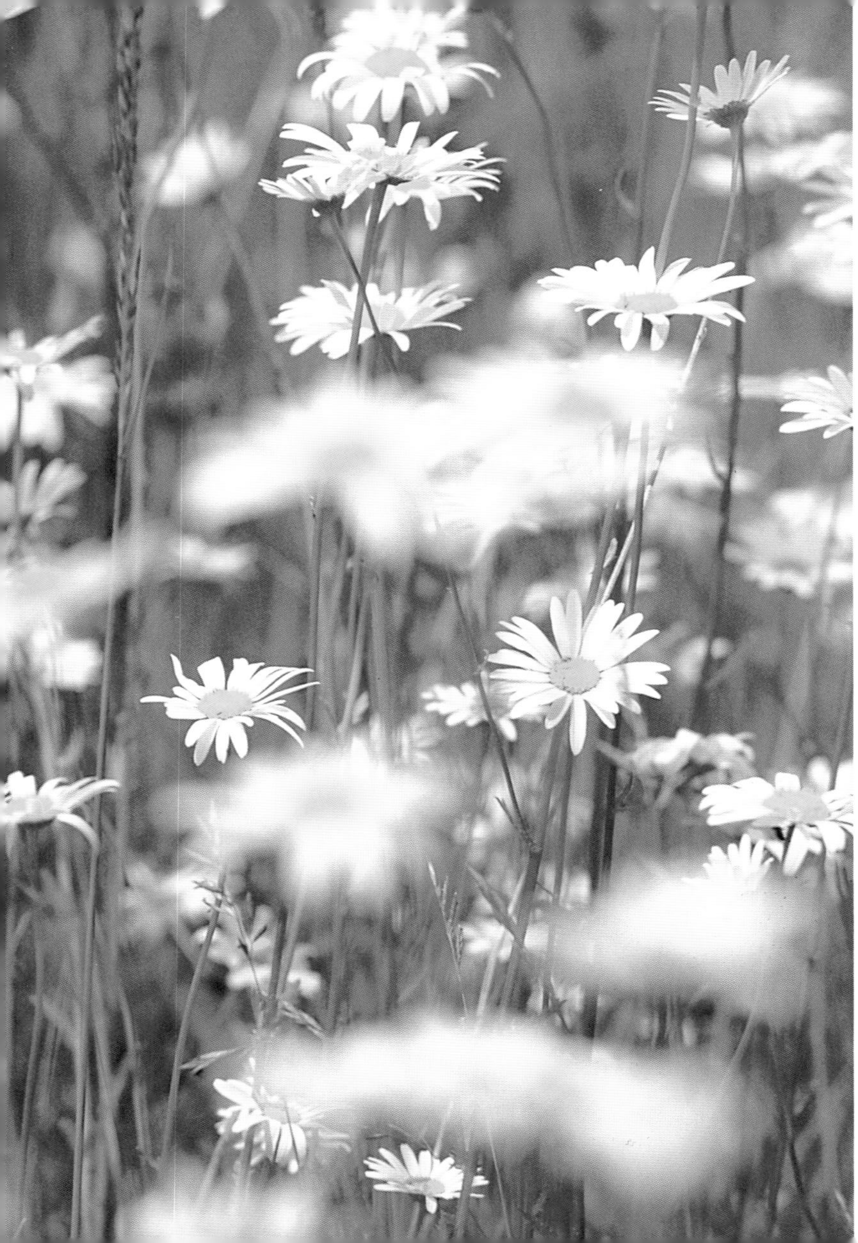

Blodau ym Mai, gorau na bai
Flowers in May, better away

Bid fyw march a gnöith wellt Mai
The horse that nibbles the grass of May will live long

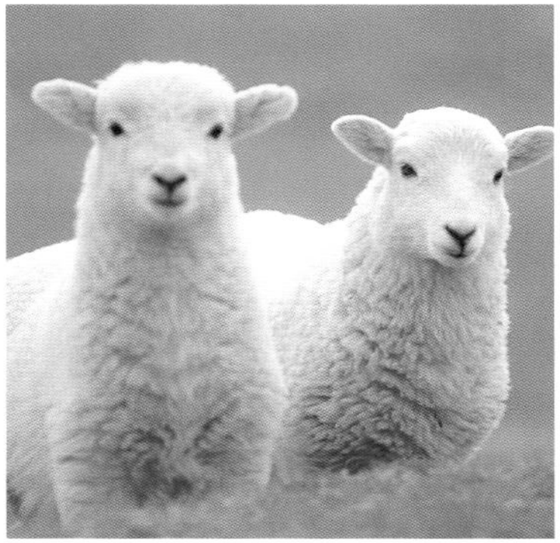

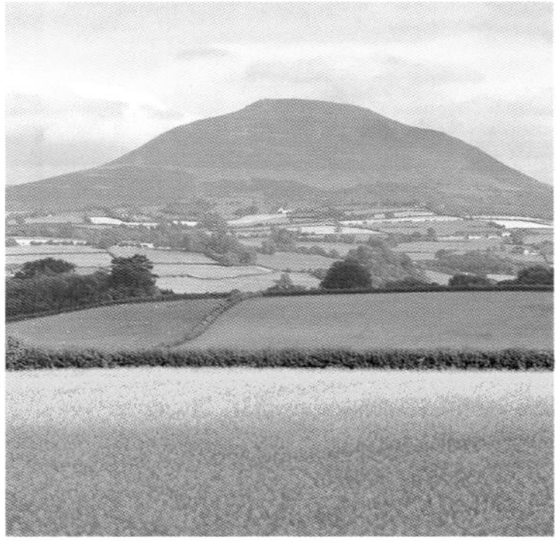

Mehefin heulog a wna fedel fochddwyreog
A sunny June will bring an early reaping party

Mis Mehefin, gwych os daw
Peth yn sych a pheth yn law
June is ideal, if partly dry and
partly wet

Awst os ceir o anian sych, a wna i Gymro ganu'n wych
A fine August will make a Welshman sing well

Tri pheth a ffynna ar des - gwenith, gwenyn a mes
Three things that flourish in warmth - wheat, bees and acorns

Gwanwyn llaith, cynhaeaf maith
A damp spring brings an ample harvest

12 | As we have always had a reputation for singing well, the hills surely must have been alive with the sound of music after a fine August. Eight hundred years ago Giraldus Cambrensis described our singing:

'When they sing together to make music, the Welsh sing their traditional songs, not in unison, as is done elsewhere, but in parts, in many modes and modulations.

When a choir gathers to sing, which happens often in this country, you will hear as many different parts and voices as there are performers, all joining together in the end to produce a single organic harmony and melody in the soft sweetness of B flat. Even more remarkable, small children sing in parts and tiny babies do so too, from the moment they stop screaming and begin to sing.'

What is now called All Hallows by the Christian Church was formerly the Celtic New Year, a time when the spirits of the dead could mix freely with those of the living. St. John's Eve was also the Midsummer festival, a supernatural period in Wales when people could cast spells to see who they were going to marry.

Haf hyd Galan
Gaeaf hyd Ŵyl Ifan
Summer until All Hallows Eve
Winter until St. John's Eve

Po decaf y bore, hacraf yr ucher
The finer the morning, the uglier the evening

Ucher a ddaw gan ddrycin
Evening will come with bad weather

Blwyddyn gneuog, blwyddyn leuog
Blwyddyn o eira, blwyddyn o lawndra
A nutty year, a lousy year
A snowy year, a year of abundance

Erbyn nos y mae canmol diwrnod teg
Praise a fine day at night

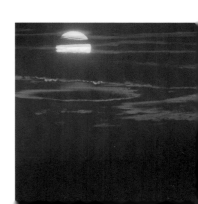

SERCH A PHRIODAS / LOVE AND MARRIAGE

Common to most societies is the offering of gifts during courtship as a token of affection. For hundreds of years, young men in Wales carved love-spoons for their sweethearts. The practice died out during the Industrial Revolution, but the spoons are still made commercially and by those competing in eisteddfodau. Perhaps because of the personal message that each spoon was meant to convey, very little has been written on the subject.

Nid brenhiniaeth ond serch, nid ynfydrwydd ond traserch
Love is the only sovereign, infatuation is the only folly

Tri anhyborth serchog - nos fer lawiog, drws gwichiedig, a gwraig anhunog ymgeingar
The three restraints of love - a short, rainy night, a squeaky door and a sleepless, bickering woman

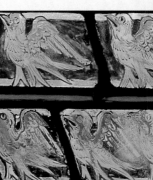

A garer a welir o bell
A loved one is spotted from a distance

Cariad a dyr drwy bob rhwystr
Love overcomes all obstacles

Cof gan bawb a gâr
Everyone remembers the one he loves

Mae brân i bob brân
For every crow there is a crow

Bedd awen gwely priodas
The marriage bed is the grave of the muse

Heb wraig, heb ymryson
Without wife, without strife

Gwell hir weddwdod na drwg briod
Better a long widowhood than a bad marriage

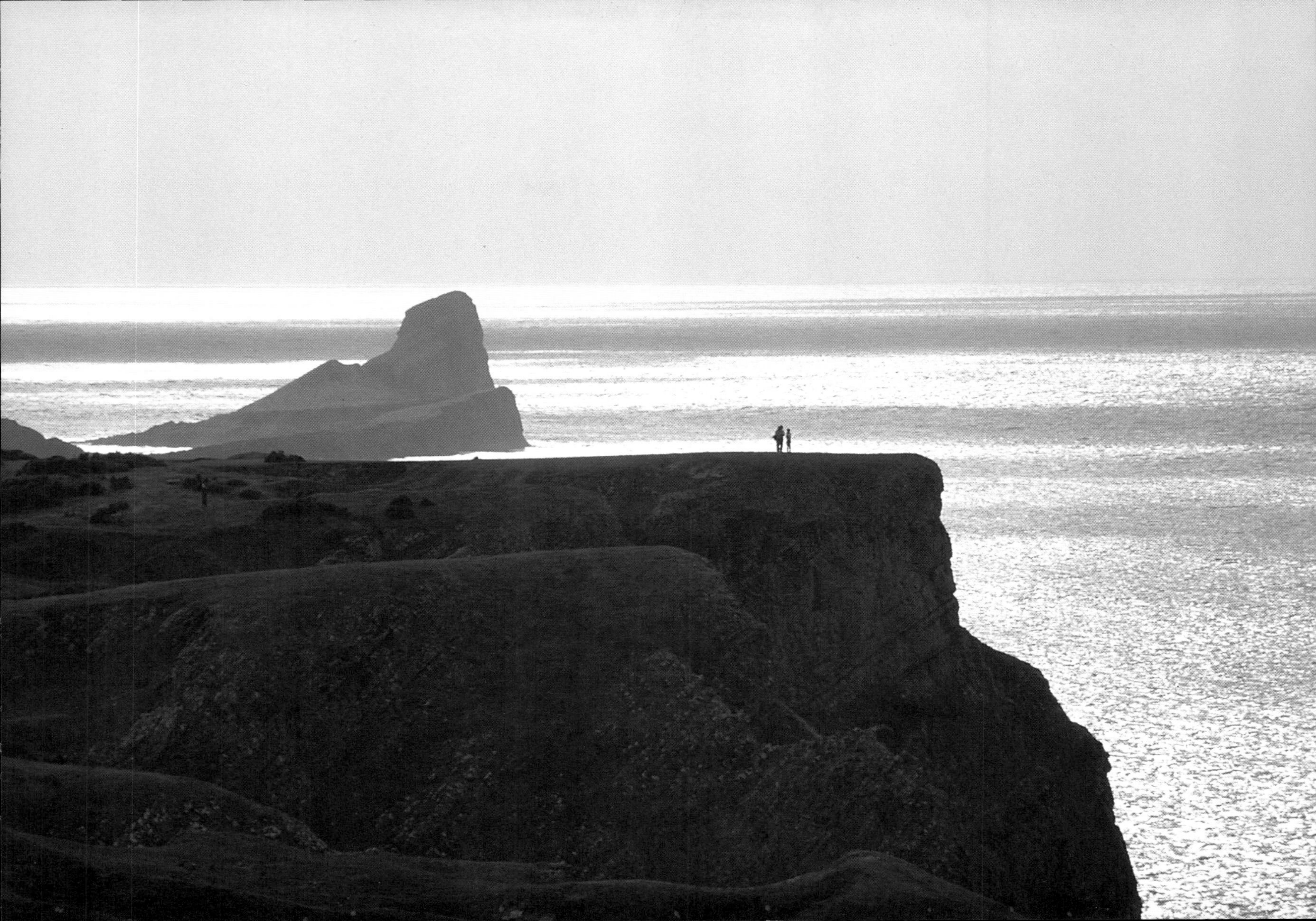

Na châr yr arian, ond câr lle bo arian
Do not love money but love where there is money

Ni bu ry-gu na bu ry-gas
There was never anything that was thoroughly loved, that was not also thoroughly hated

Ni fydd hunog serchog byth
A lover is never sleepy

Trech serch na chawr
Love is stronger than a giant

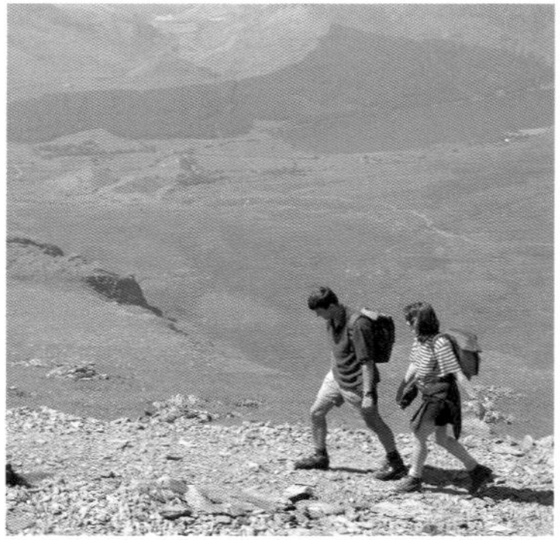

Meddwl serchog, syberw sydd
Loving thoughts are proud

Ni ddaw cof i chwegr ei bod yn waudd
A mother-in-law forgets that she was a daughter-in-law

Tew y beiau lle tenau'r cariad
Faults are thick where love is thin

Pe gwelai serch ei wendid, fe drengai gan ofn
If love could see its weakness, it would die of fright

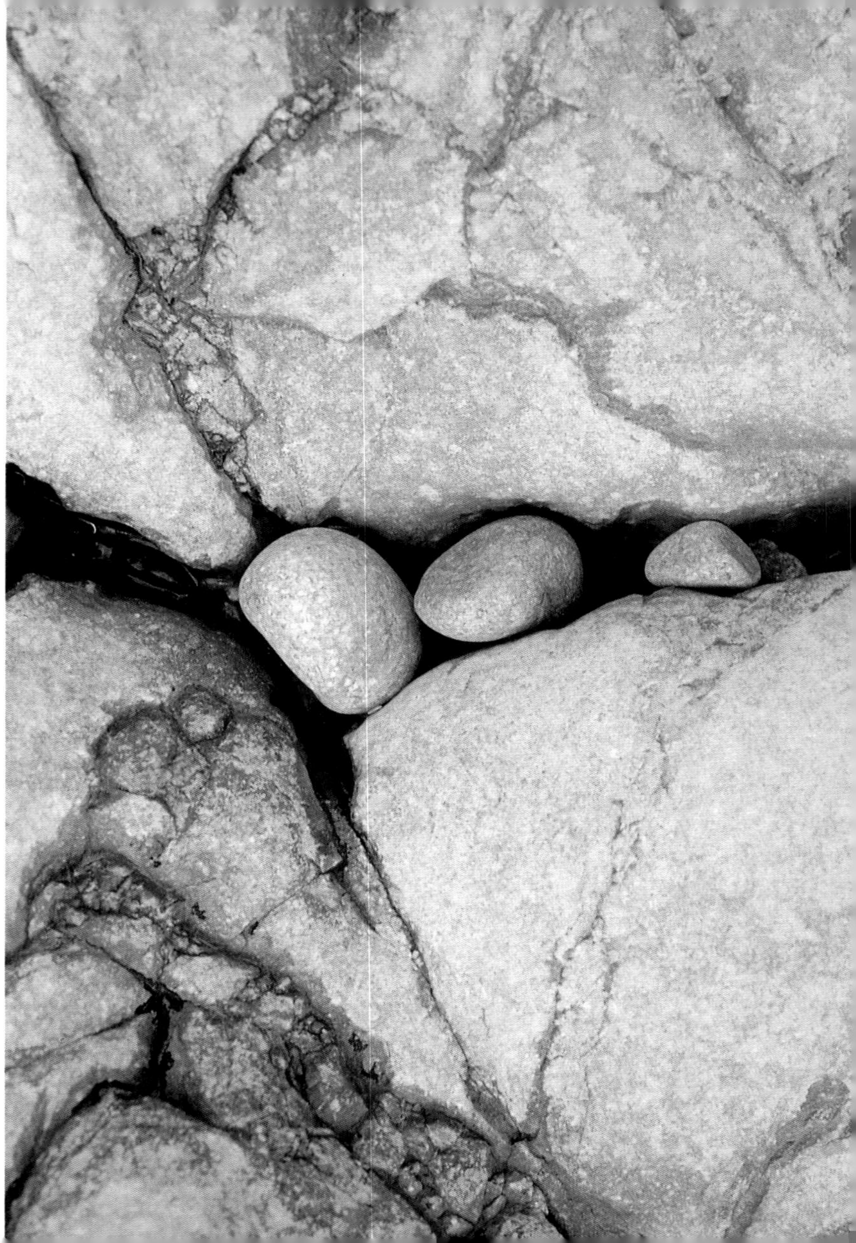

DUW A'R EGLWYS / GOD AND THE CHURCH

As with the other Celtic nations, religion has always been very important to the Welsh, whether it is Christianity or the earlier religion of the Druids. In fact, the power of the Druids was such that the Romans decided to massacre them on the Isle of Angelsey, which was their headquarters. Tacitus described the slaughter in some detail.

Nevertheless, many Druids must have escaped, because one of the disagreements between the Celtic and Roman Churches was that the British priests shaved their heads in the way of the Druids. The Christian Church then continued to use the sacred sites of the earlier religion, planting the yew trees that were also sacred to the Celts. Even some of the standing stones were later recycled for Christian use.

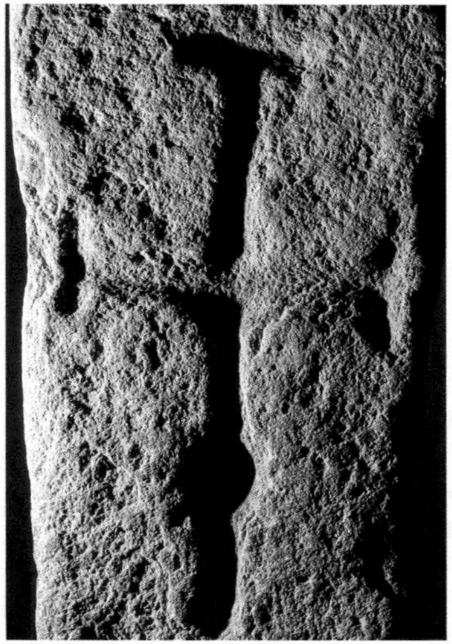

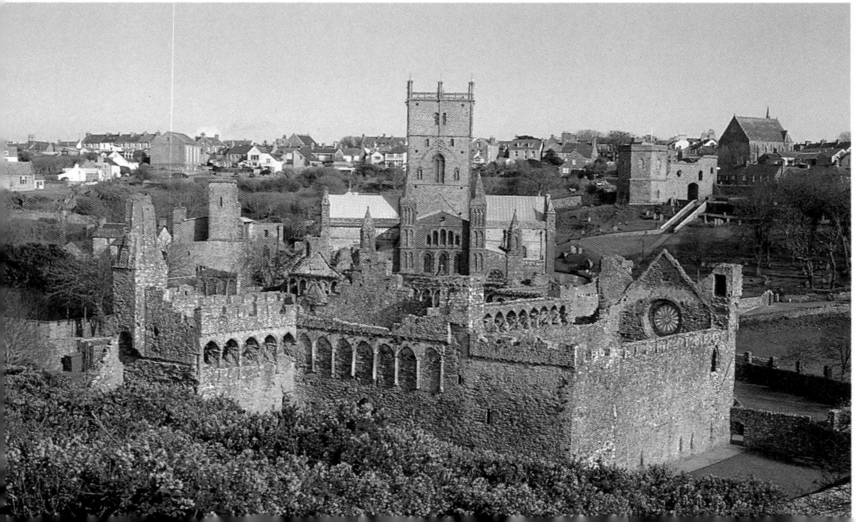

During what is known in the rest of Europe as the Dark Ages, the Celtic saints emerged, spreading knowledge and hope. This was our 'Age of the Saints'. In fact, there were so many that it has been suggested that Wales and Ireland have more saints between them than the rest of the world put together!

Whether this is true or not, it does underline the great significance of spirituality in our lives, right up to this century. The proliferation of chapels built in the last century only serves to underline this point. And we should not forget that the oldest cathedral settlement in Britain is St. David's in west Wales. Its founder in the middle of the 6th century was Dewi Sant / St. David, who is the patron saint of Wales.

CHRIST
DIED
FOR
OUR SINS
ACCORDING to the SCRIPTURES

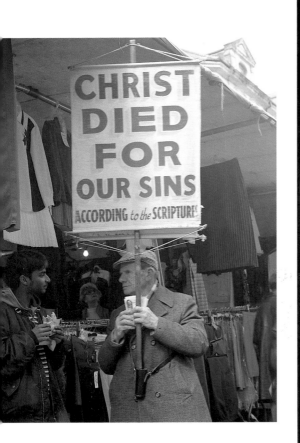

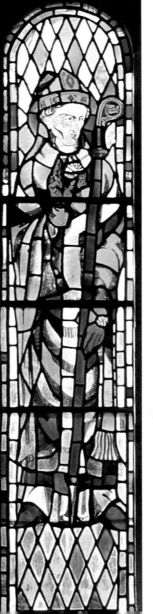

Pan gysgo pawb ar gylched, ni chwsg Duw pan rydd gwared
When everyone else is sleeping in his bed, God will sleep not when he redeems

Nesaf i'r eglwys, pellaf o baradwys
The nearer to church, the farther from paradise

Nid llai y crefydd yn unman na lle bo mwyaf y dadlu amdano
There is no less religion anywhere than where it is argued about

Nid cof gan yr offeiriad iddo fod yn glochydd
The priest does not remember being a bell-ringer

A fynno Duw a fydd
What God wills will be

Cofia dy Dduw pan drewych
Remember your God when you sneeze

Da yw Duw, a hir yw byth
God is good and eternity is long

Duw a fedd, dyn a lefair
Man talks but God rules

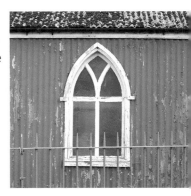

'*Dyn a chwennych, Duw a ran*
Man desires, God distributes

Cas dyn yma, cas Duw fry
Those who hate their fellow man will hate God

Lle bo eglwys gan Dduw bydd capel gan y diafol
Where God has a church the devil will have a chapel

Hir yr erys Duw cyn taro, ond llwyr ei ddial ef pan ddelo
God's retribution is long in coming, but when it does his revenge is total

Rhaid wrth allwedd dda i fynd i baradwys
A good key is needed to enter Paradise

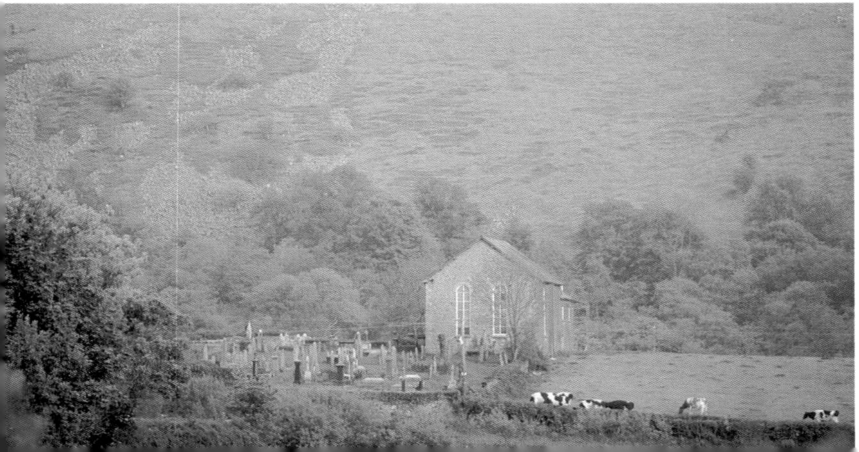

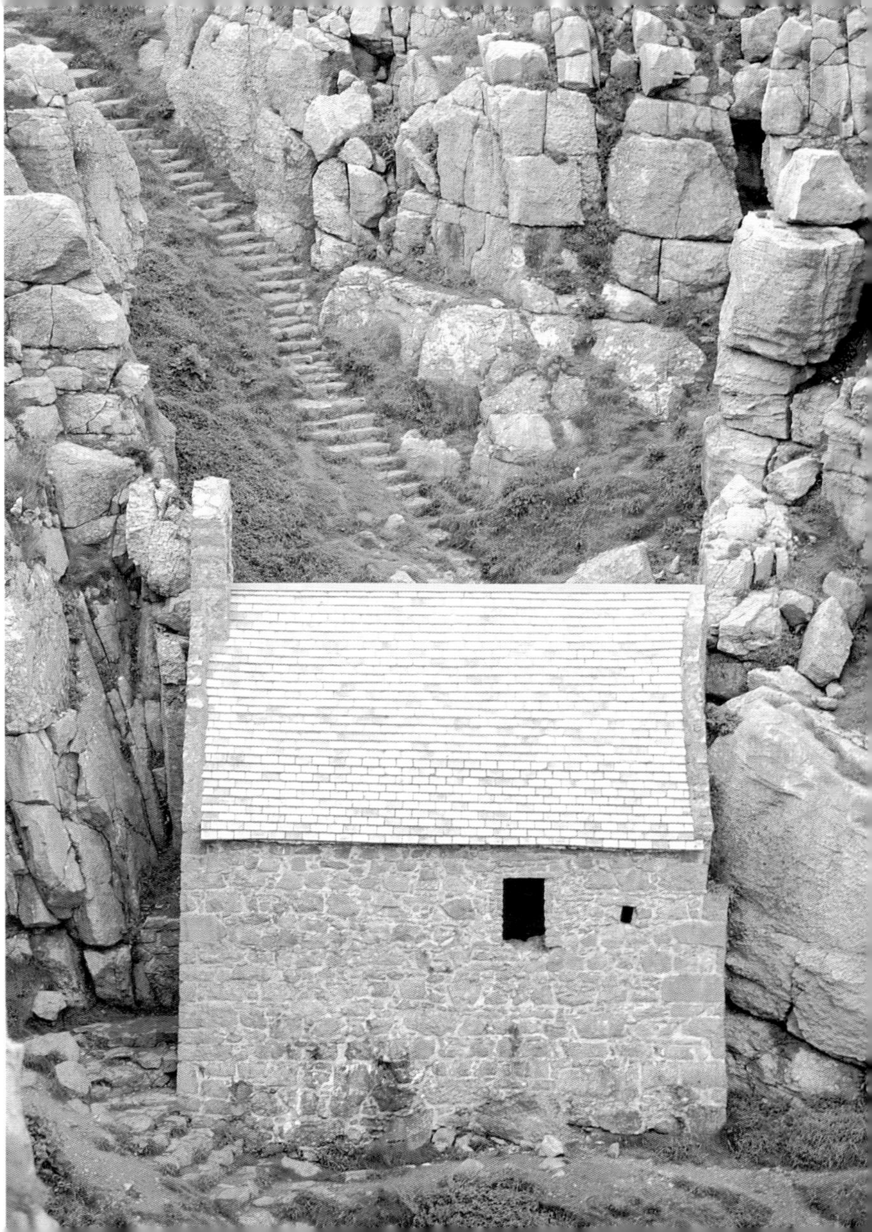

'*Nid dan chwibanu mae mynd i'r nef*
It is not by whistling that one goes to Heaven

Ond Duw nid oes benadur
No sovereign but God

Gwasanaeth Duw yw gwneuthur iawn,
Nid gweddïo bore a nawn
Doing right is the service of God,
not simply praying morning and evening

Nid tref ond nef
No home but heaven

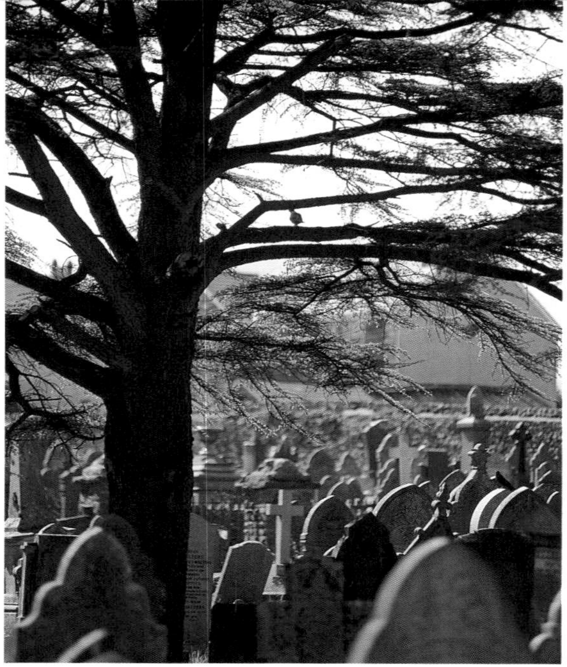

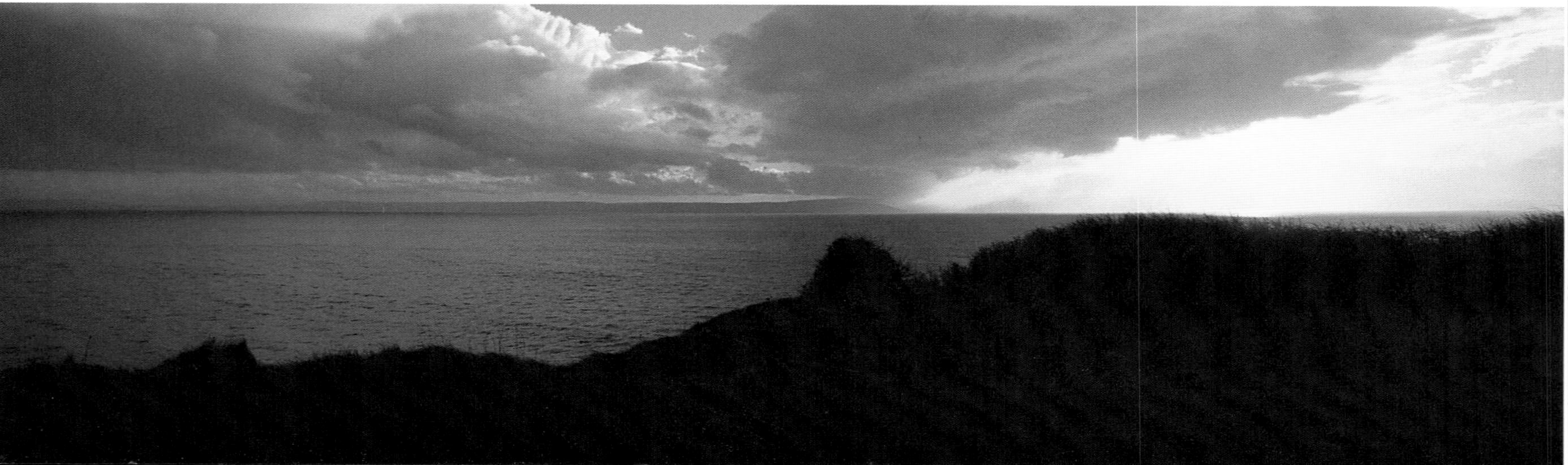

In 1095 Pope Urban II unleashed an army of princes, knights and commoners from all over Europe against the Arab world. Wales naturally played a part in this; Giraldus Cambrensis accompanied Archbishop Baldwin of Canterbury in 1188 around Wales recruiting men. He then wrote about it in his Itinerarium Kambriae.

The Crusades continued for almost another four hundred years after Archbishop Baldwin's visit to Wales. One visible effect of the Crusades was the design of castles like Caernarfon, which were influenced by the architecture of Constantinople.

Aed glew i gynnwrf cad, Duw a'i differ
Let a brave man go into the tumult of battle, God will protect him

Nid derwydd eithr o enwad, nid derwydd ond Duw
The only true Druid is God

Tri phrif ofynion Duw: cariad, cyfiawnder, ac ufudd-dod
The three main requirements of God: love, justice and obedience

O fôr ac o fynydd ac o waelod afonydd, y danfon Duw dda i ddedwydd
From the sea and mountain, from the depth of rivers, God sends goodness to the contented

Offeren pawb yn ei galon
Everyone's mass is in his heart

Tri pheth sydd o godi'n fore - iechyd, cyfoeth a santeiddrwydd
Three things come from early rising - health, wealth and holiness

Crefydd a ladd y drwg; ni wna moes ond ei guddio
Religion kills evil; morality only hides it

Byrhoedlog digasog saint
Short-lived is he who is hateful to saints

Y DIAFOL / THE DEVIL

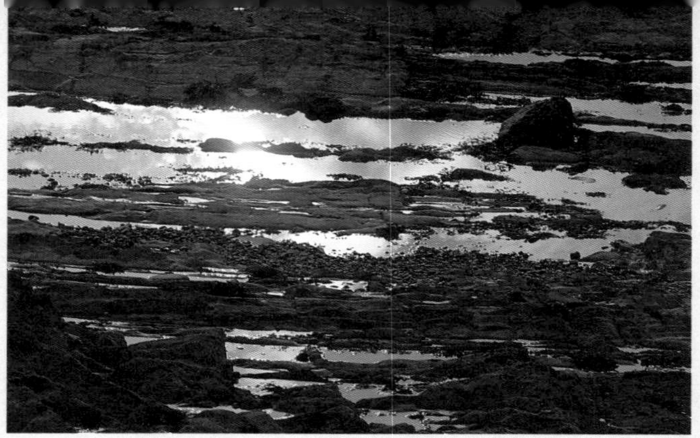

The popular picture of the Devil, with horns and cloven hooves, has nothing to do with any description from the Bible: it is rather a picture of the Celtic god Cernunnos (the horned one). It was quite natural for the new religion of Christianity to decry the old one and to turn the old gods into malevolent beings.

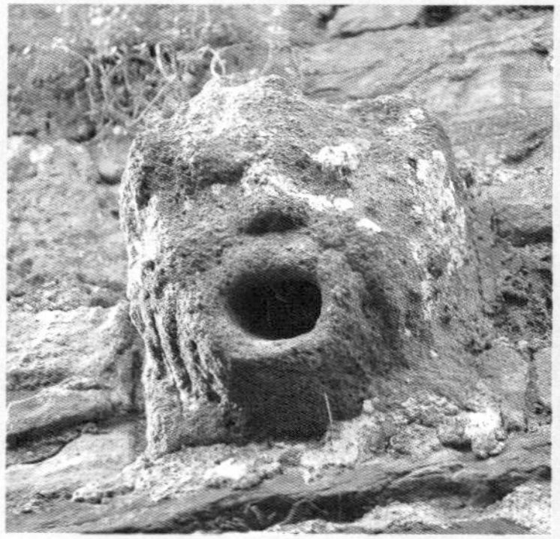

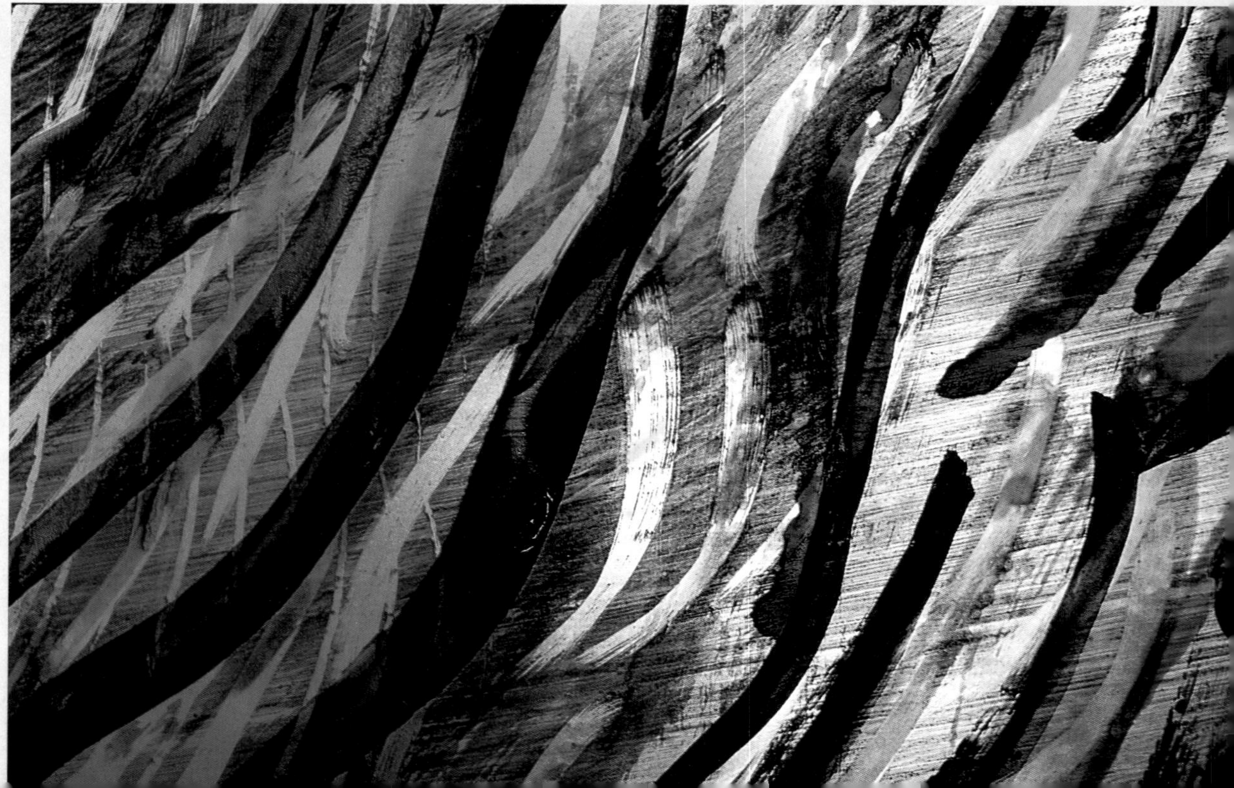

Ymrith y drwg ar lun daioni
Evil will disguise itself as goodness

Tri nod cywir sydd ar ddyn y diawl: ac nis gall ymddiheuro ag hwynt: ei air, ei olwg, ei ymodi
Three signs which a man of the Devil cannot hide: his word, his appearance and his actions

Gŵr diog yw llawffon y diawl
A lazy man is the Devil's walking stick

Gwna dda dros ddrwg, uffern ni'th ddwg
Repay evil with good and hell will not claim you

Mae'r diawl yn dda tra ei sidaner
The Devil is good whilst being flattered

Mae'r diawl yn dda tra ei sidaner
The Devil is good whilst being flattered

Rhaid llwy hir i fwyta gyda'r diawl
If you eat with the Devil you need a long spoon

Nid oes ar uffern ond eisiau ei threfnu
The only thing hell needs is to be organised

Nid eir i annwfn ond unwaith
Only once does one go to the otherworld

23

Fe ddaw'r dyn drwg o feddwl amdano
The evil one will come if you think about him

Ychydig a wneid am y nef, pe diffoddid uffern
Little would be done about heaven if hell fire were extinguished

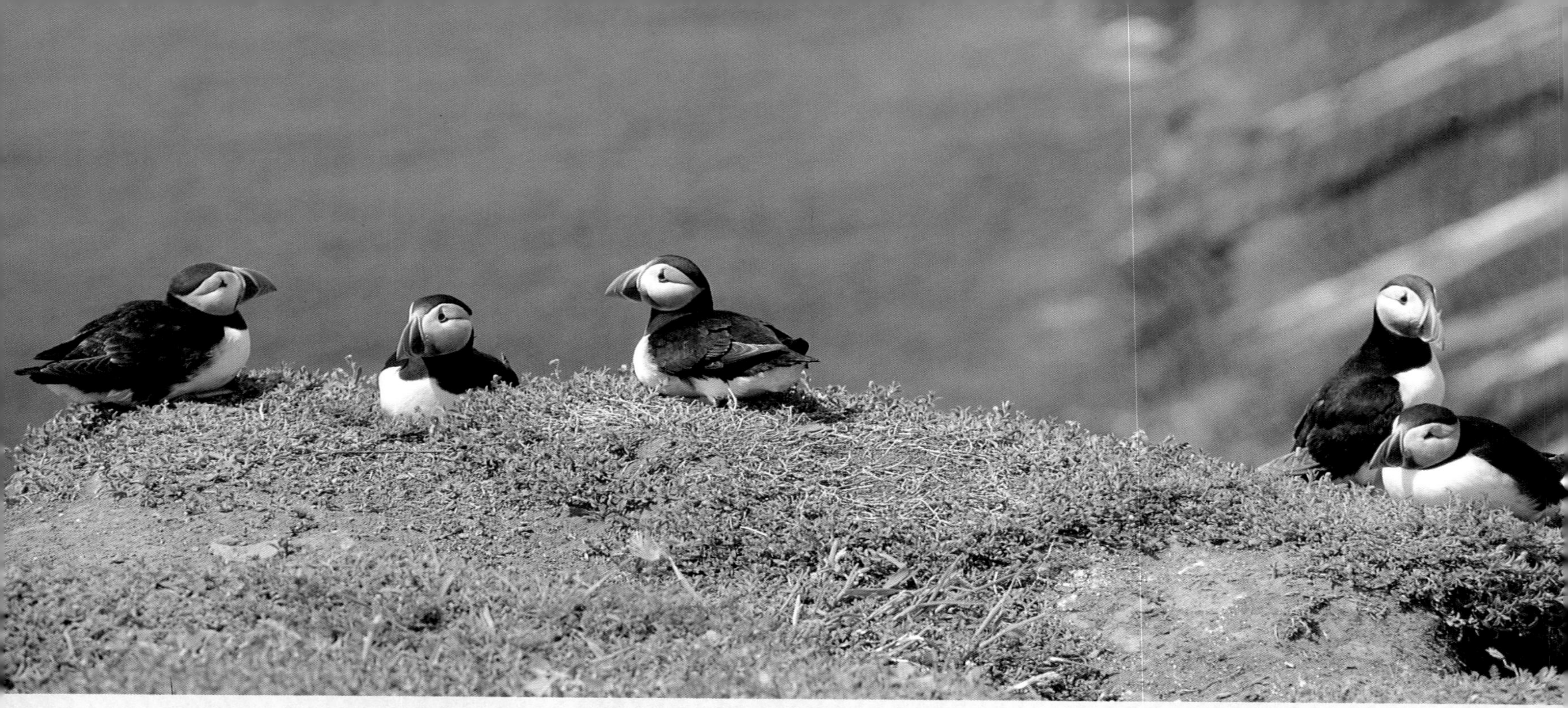

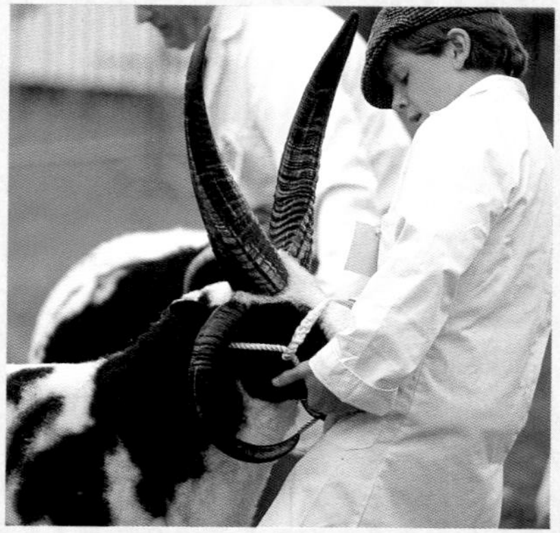

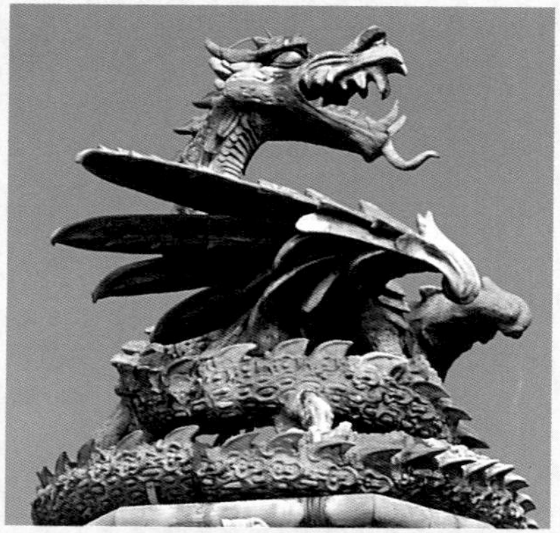

ANIFEILIAID / ANIMALS

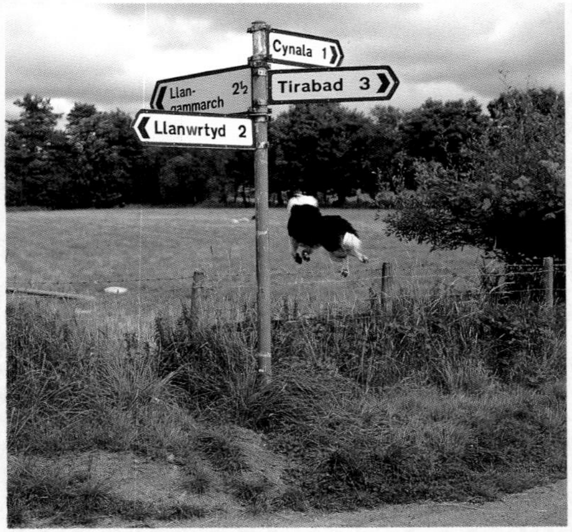
Cynala 1
Tirabad 3
Llan-
gammarch 2½
Llanwrtyd 2

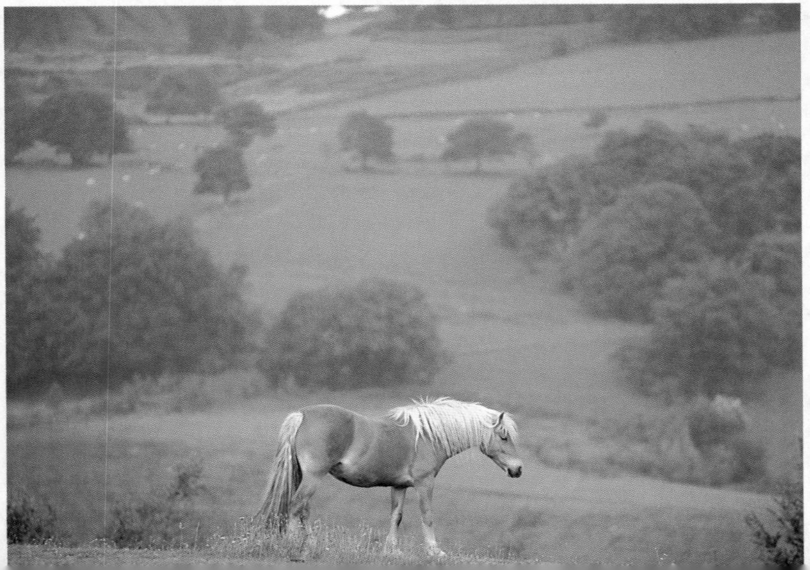

How many children today have regular contact with animals? A researcher found that a high percentage of children in New York thought that milk came from a factory, and it is quite probable that many children would refuse to eat eggs if they really knew where they came from. Never have we had less direct contact with other members of the animal kingdom. However, we can see from these proverbs that certain animals were once perceived to have specific characteristics, just as humans do.

Many of the Celtic gods were named after animals. Brân means crow in Welsh; Arthur, our mythical king, has his root in arth, the Welsh word for bear. Everyday Welsh names like Bleddyn and Llewelyn are related to the wolf and lion respectively.

For hundreds of years the Welsh economy relied to a great extent on the export of animals into England. Drovers walked their cattle and sheep for miles over the hills to the English markets and fairs. Unfortunately, the drovers themselves could rarely afford to eat the meat they were driving: their staple diet was normally oats. The railways brought an end to their trade, with only a few drovers surviving into the beginning of the twentieth century.

Welsh dogs like corgis (cor=dwarf ci=dog) have become sought after all over the world. Followers of royal families will know that Queen Elizabeth II's favourite dogs are corgis.

Sheepdogs have probably been with us as long as we have been keeping sheep. Anyone who has attended sheepdog trials in Wales will know how essential they are and will have seen the special relationship between shepherd and dog.

Nid cywir ond ci
No fidelity like that of a dog

Gormod o bwdin a dag gi
Too much pudding will choke a dog

Annos dy gi, ac na ddos ganddo
Set your dog on but don't go with it

Mae hen gof gan hen gi
An old dog has an old memory

Ci yn udo noson ole, newydd drwg ddaw yn y bore
A baying dog on a moonlit night, mournful news in the morning light

Na sang ar droed ci chwerw
Do not tread on an angry dog's paw

Adar o'r unlliw, hedant i'r unlle
Birds of a feather flock together

Nid budr ond hwyad
Nought as dirty as the duck

Ni chwyn yr iâr fod y gwalch yn glaf
The hen won't complain that the hawk is ill

Crefydd iâr wrth ei gylfin
The hen's beak her mind doth speak

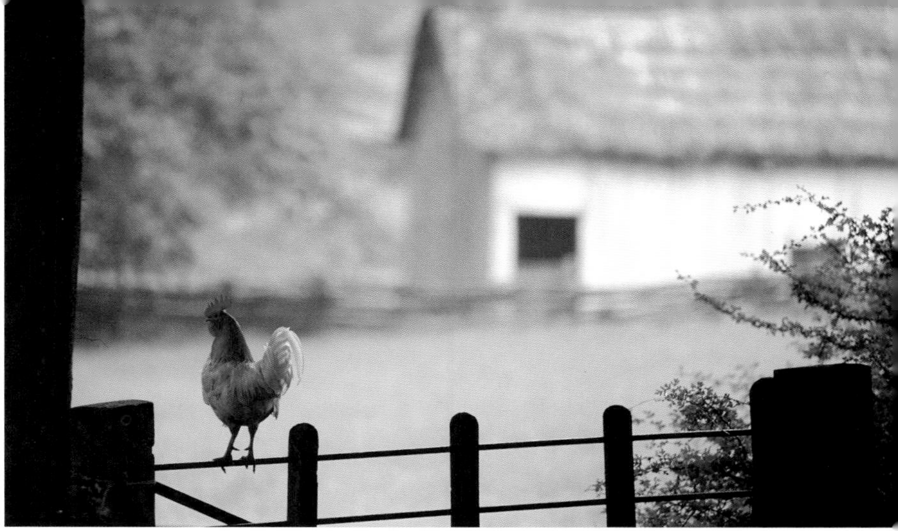

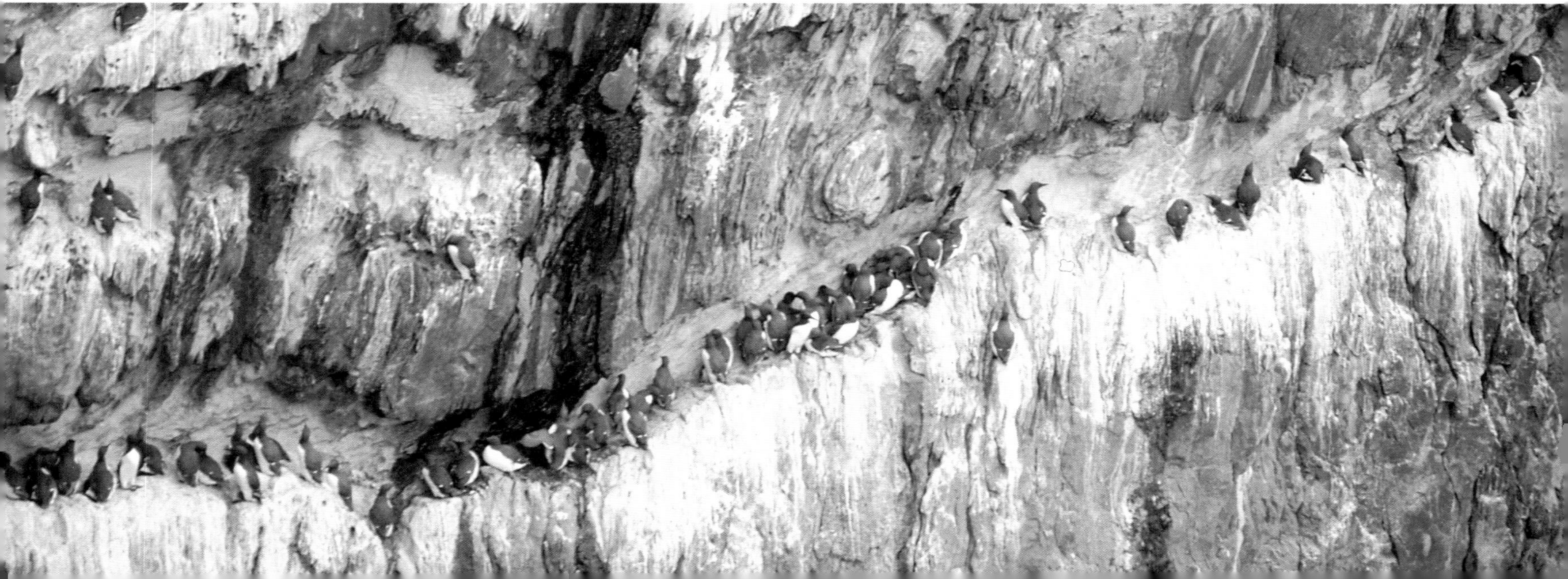

YR
HEN BEN TARW

Welsh Black Cattle were already present when the Romans arrived in Britain. They are ideally suited for living on harsh high ground like Snowdonia, as they can survive on very little. They grow a thick coat during the cold winter months, then lose it when the summer comes.

Cu anner wedi praidd
The heifer is only valued when the herd is gone

Tarw gwibiog, ni wêl ei fuches ei hun
A roving bull doesn't see its own herd

Buwch o ryw, ceffyl o gymysg
A pedigree cow, a horse of mixed breed

Godrir buwch o'i phen
A cow is milked from its head

Nid hawdd yr ardd yr ych heb ei gymar
It is not easy for an ox to plough without its partner

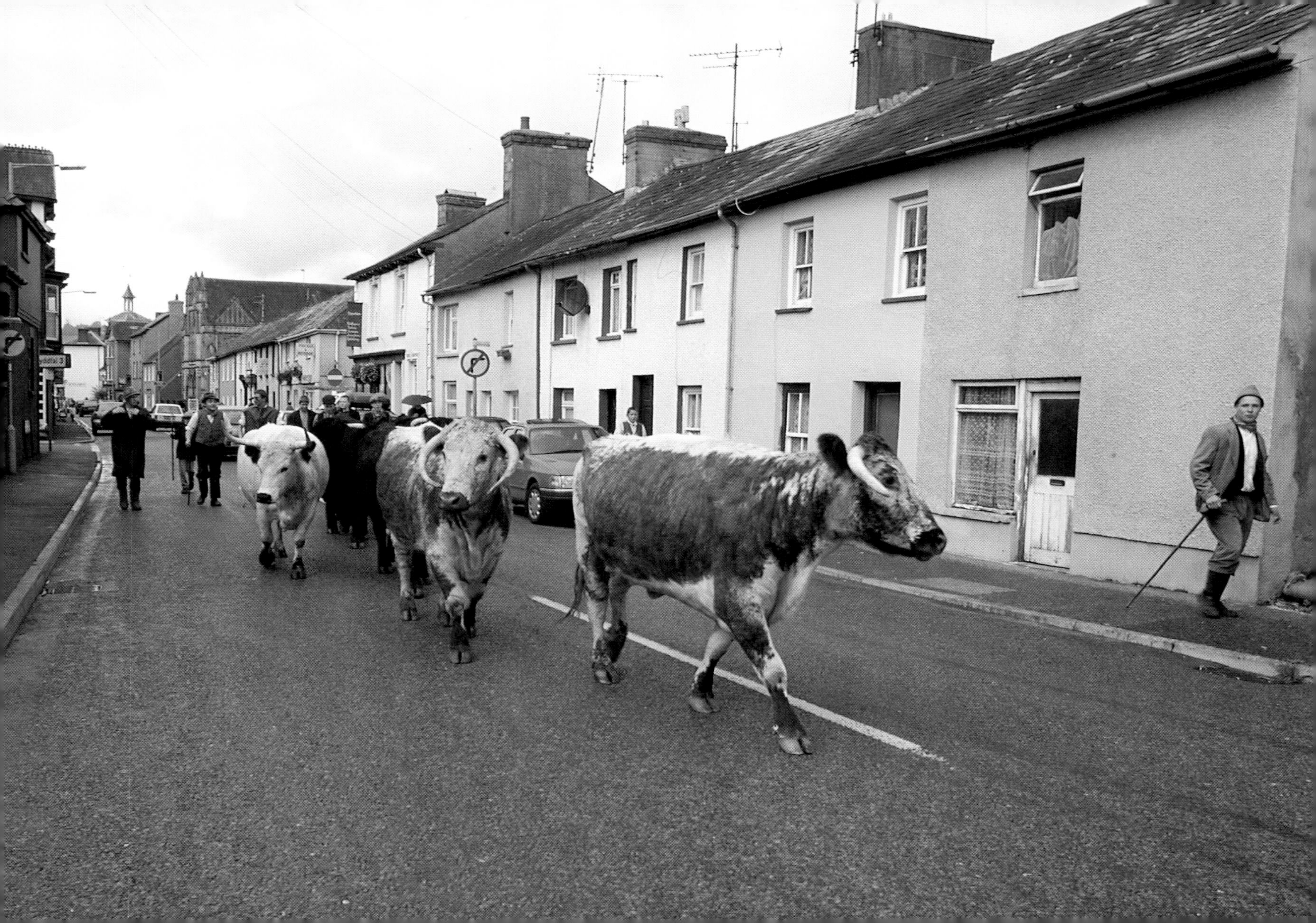

Wolves disappeared from Wales in the seventeenth century, after constant persecution throughout Britain. It is reputed that the last wolf in Wales was shot at Gregrina, near Builth Wells.

There were many ways of encouraging people to kill them - for instance, instead of criminals being sent to prison, they were allowed to remain free as long as they killed a certain number of wolves every year. The government also paid people for every wolf they killed. These notorious animals obviously played an important role in the fears of people throughout Europe.

Cyfaill blaidd, bugail diog
A lazy shepherd is the wolf's friend

Ys ef y blaidd y bugail
The wolf is often the shepherd

Llafar oen, calon blaidd
A lamb's bleat, a wolf's heart

Po amlaf fo'r bleiddiau, gwaethaf fydd i'r defaid
The more numerous the wolves, the worse it will be for the sheep

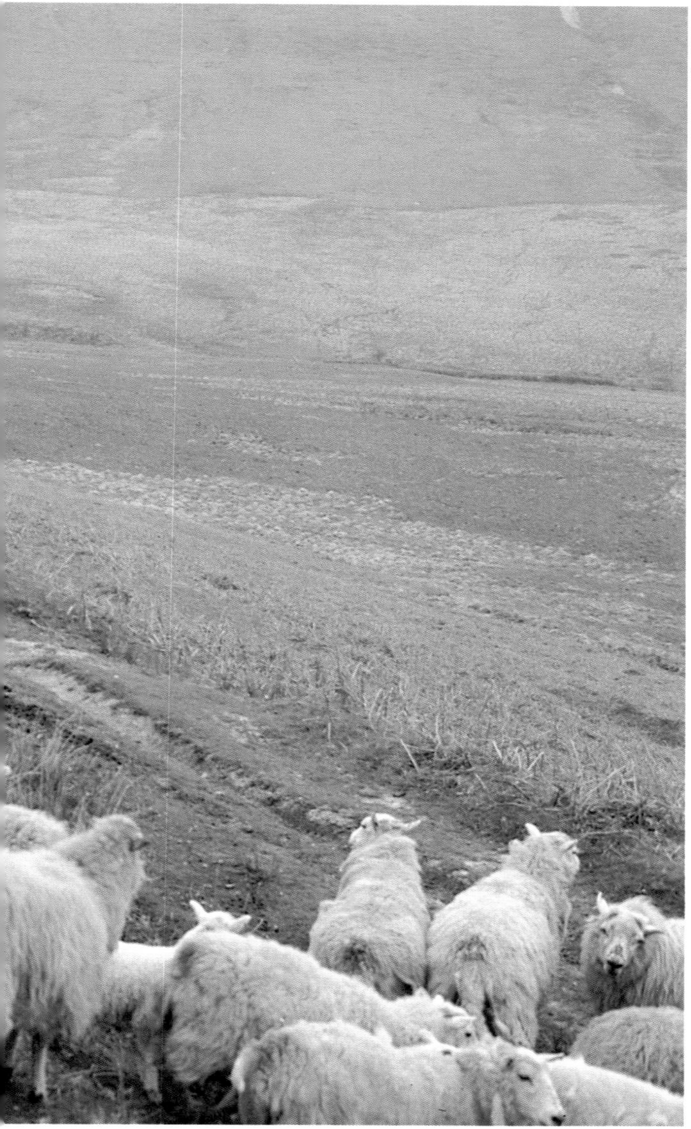

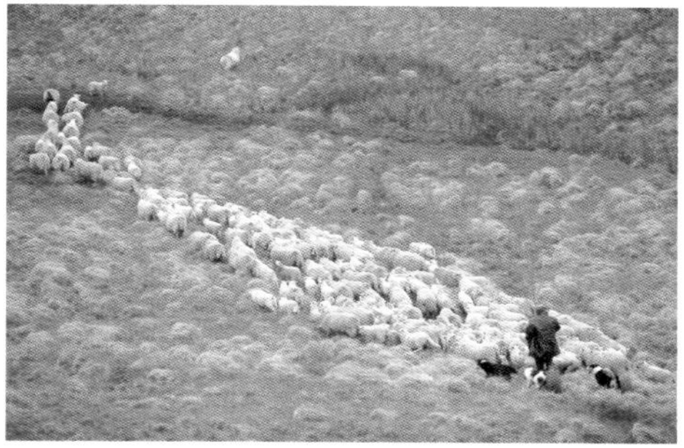

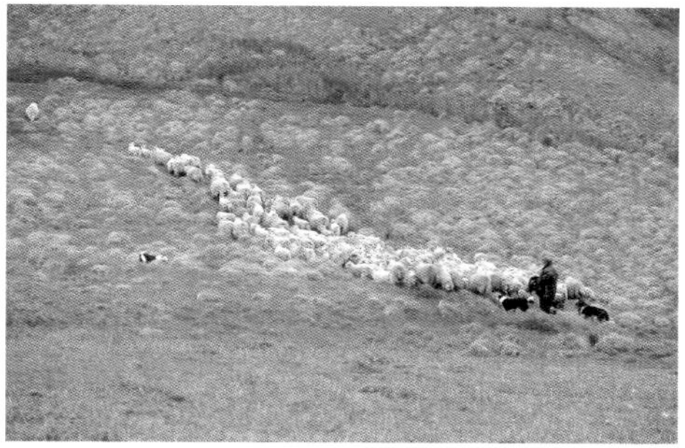

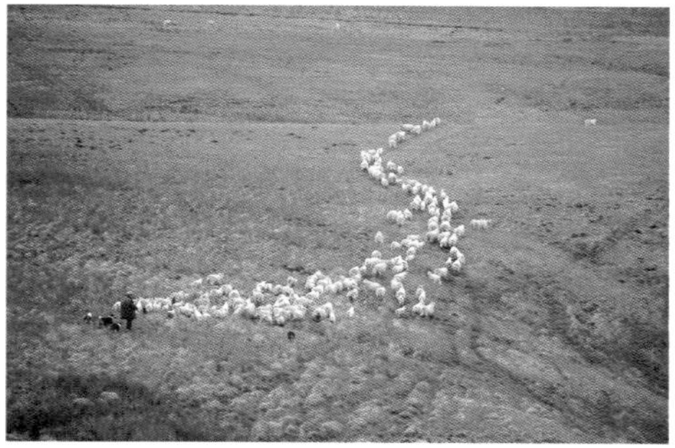

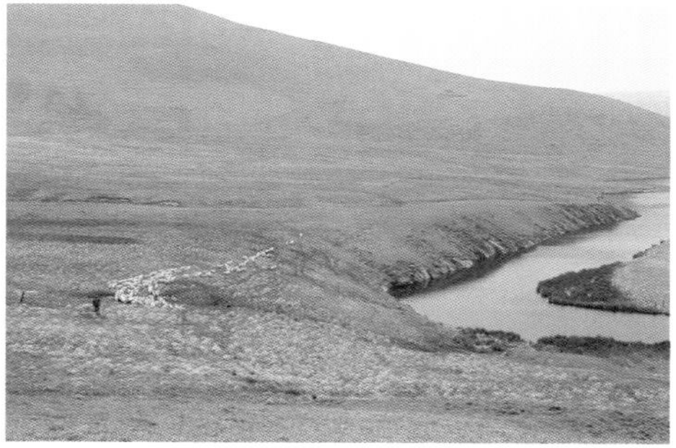

At any given time there are at least three times as many sheep as people in Wales; there are also at least ten indigenous Welsh breeds.

Yr oen yn dysgu i'r ddafad bori
The lamb teaching the ewe to graze

Diwedd hen cadw defaid
The last occupation of the elderly is to look after the sheep

Cas myharen mieri
A ram hates brambles

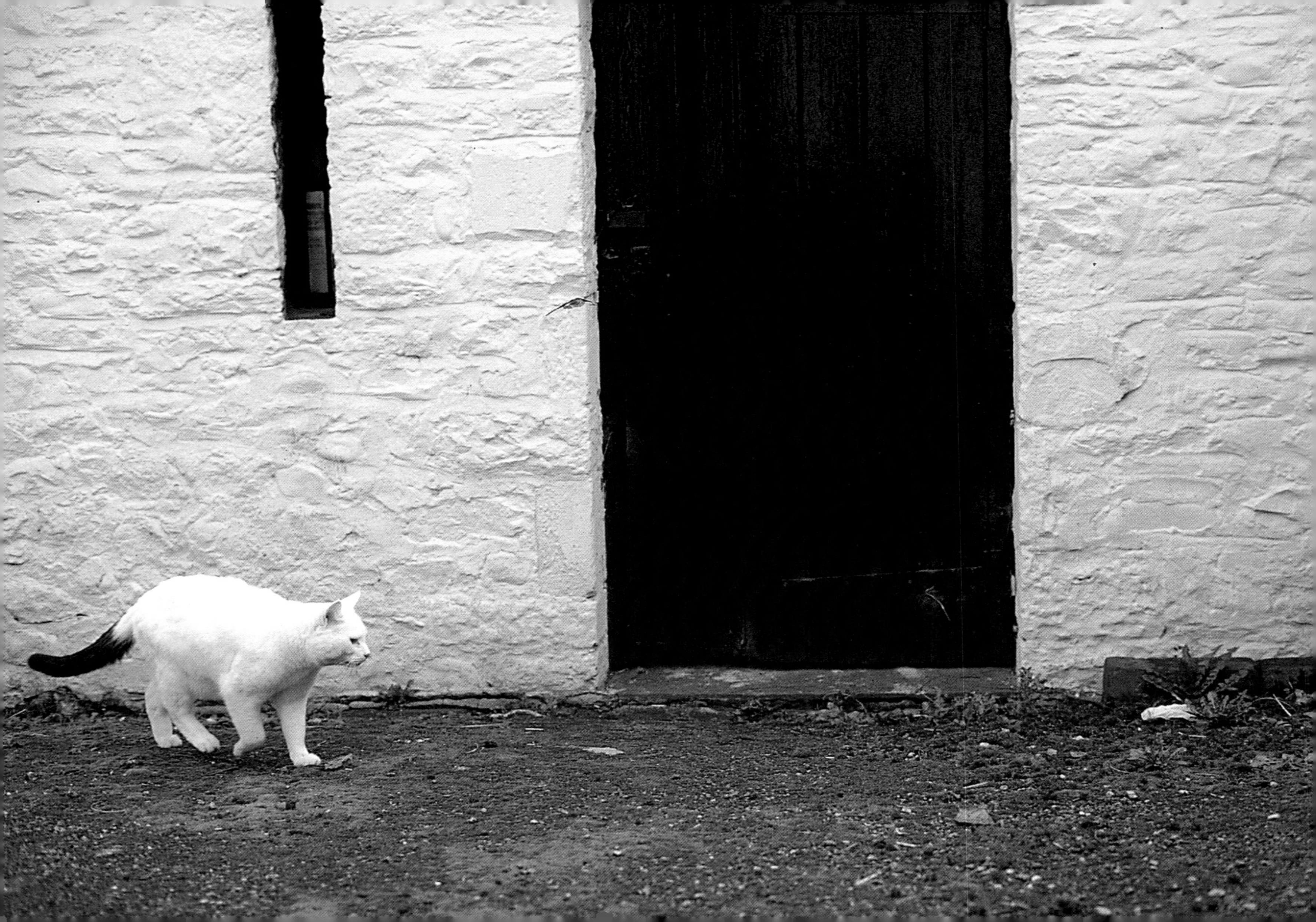

The Law of Hywel Dda, King of South Wales A.D. 936

The worth of a cat and its characteristics is this -
The worth of a kitten from the night it is born
until it shall open its eyes is one penny.
And from that time until it kills mice, two pence.
And after it kills mice, four legal pence,
and so it shall always remain.
Her characteristics are to see, to hear, to kill mice,
to have its claws complete, to rear and not devour
its young and if it is bought and be deficient in any
one of these characteristics, let one third of its worth be returned.
The worth of a cat that is killed or stolen is
determined thus; let its head be put downwards upon a
clean and even floor with its tail lifted upwards, and
thus suspended whilst wheat is poured about it until
the tip of its tail is covered - and that is to be its worth.
The worth of a common cat is four legal pence.
Whoever sells a cat is to answer for it not going a
caterwauling every moon, and that it shall not devour
its kittens, and that it shall have ears, teeth and nails
and be a good mouser.

Edwyn hen gath lefrith
An old cat knows milk

Naw byw cath
The nine lives of a cat

Wrth ymrafael yr â'r cathod ynghyd
Through quarrelling cats come together

Ŵyr y gath pa farf a lyf
The cat knows whose beard it licks

A'r ni phortho ei gath, porthed ei lygod
He who does not feed his cat will feed his mice

33

When Julius Caesar arrived in Britain in 55BC he was astounded by the expertise of the British charioteers, writing that 'The British are masters of their horses and chariots.' As soon as they could, the Romans recruited them as mercenaries into the Imperial Army. In the tenth century Hywel Dda, the King of South Wales, classified the different types of horse in Wales and their worth.

Edwyn hen farch us
An old horse knows chaff

Hir bydd march bach yn ebol
A small horse will long be called a foal

March i ddiog, ci i lwth
A horse for the lazy man, a dog for the glutton

Yn y lle ydd ymgreinio y march, ydd edy beth o'i flew
Where the horse rolls it will leave some of its hair

Buan ar farch buan i'r arch
Swift on the horse, swift to the coffin

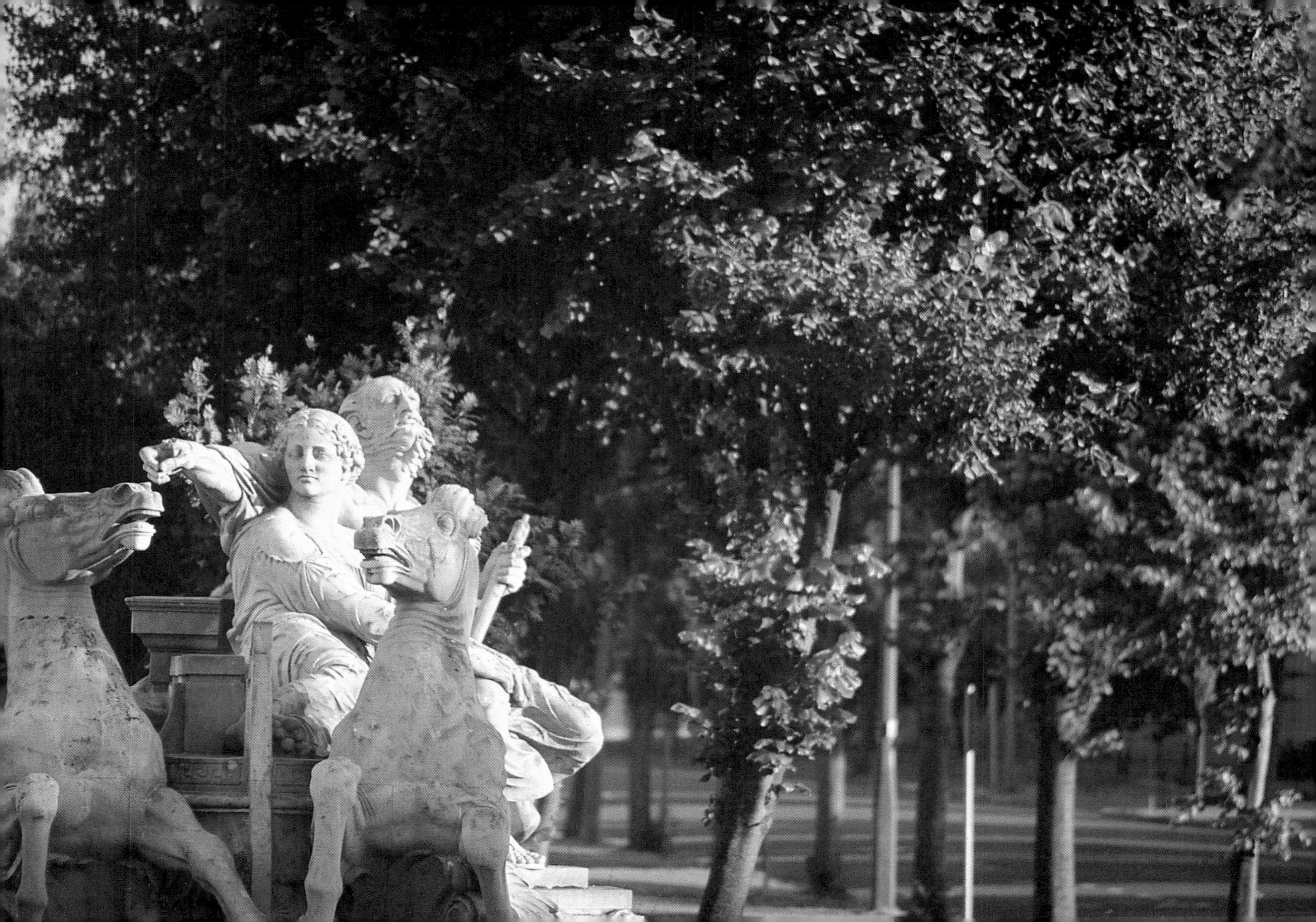

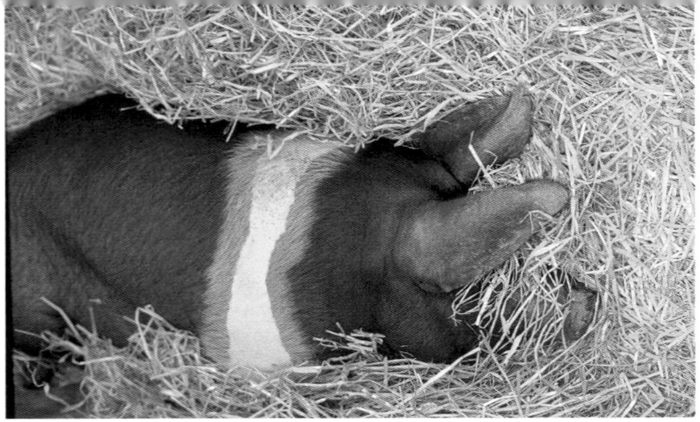

The pig was seen by the Celts as the choicest animal that could be eaten. There was even a pig-god called Moccus - and mochyn is still the Welsh word for pig.

Pob twrch a ddadredd, rhaid deallus i ddatod
Every hog can tear things up, only the clever can undo

Bendith i'r hwch biau'r bloneg
A blessing on the fat sow

Rhyw i hwch ei rhwch
A sow's nature is to grunt

A elo yn hwch yn Rhydychen, yn hwch y daw yn ôl
A sow that goes to Oxford will be a sow when she returns

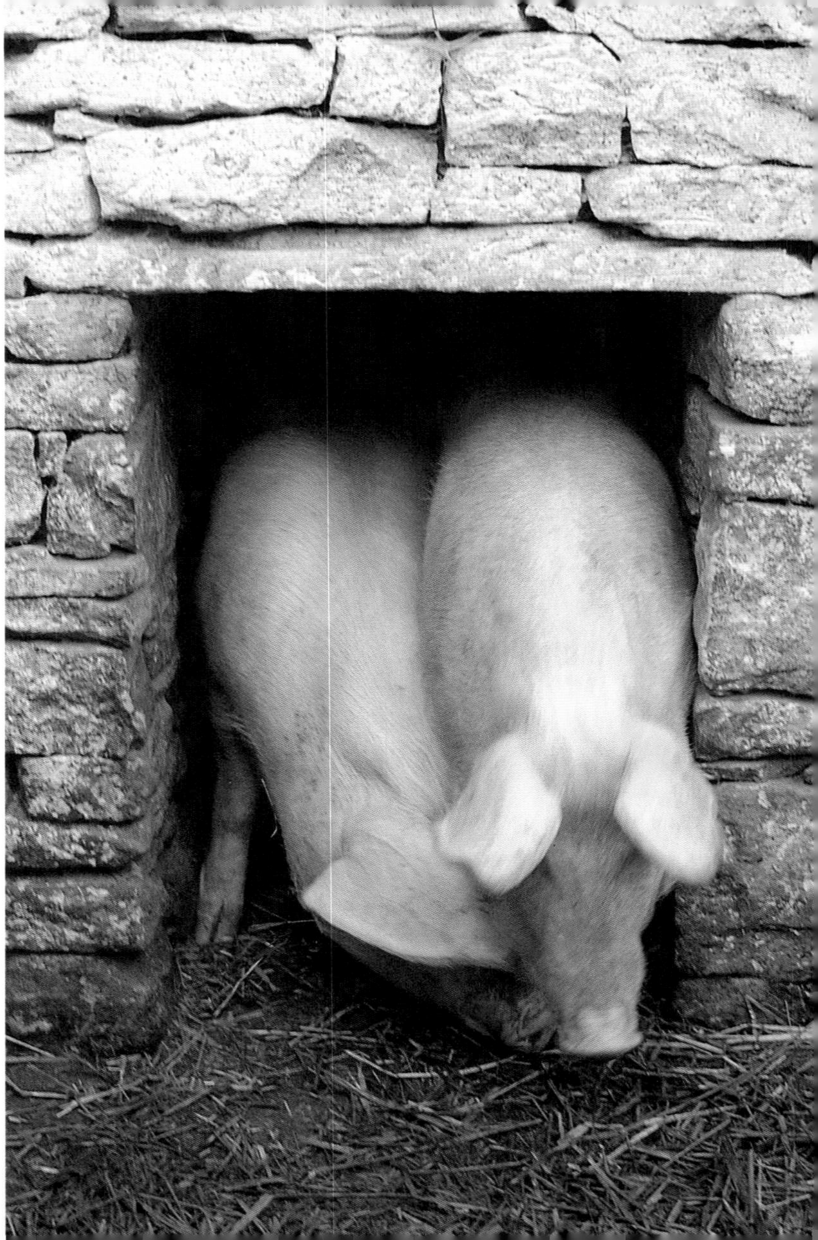

Coracles are still used on rivers like the Teifi and the Tawe for fishing salmon. This small round craft can be carried on the fisherman's shoulders because it is so light; it is then easily manipulated in the water by those with experience. The use of coracles dates back to prehistory, when even seas were crossed in them.

Nid glân ond y pysg
Nothing as clean as a fish

Po grochaf fo'r afon, lleiaf fydd o bysgod
Louder the river, fewer the fish

Llysywen mewn dwrn yw arian
Money is like an eel in the fist

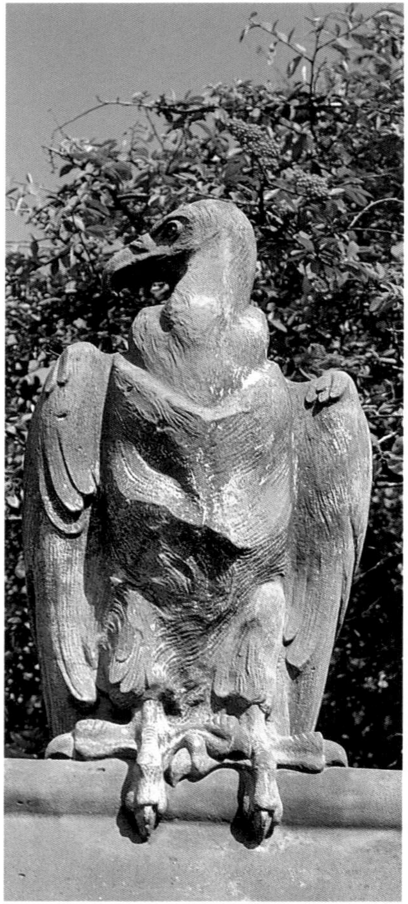

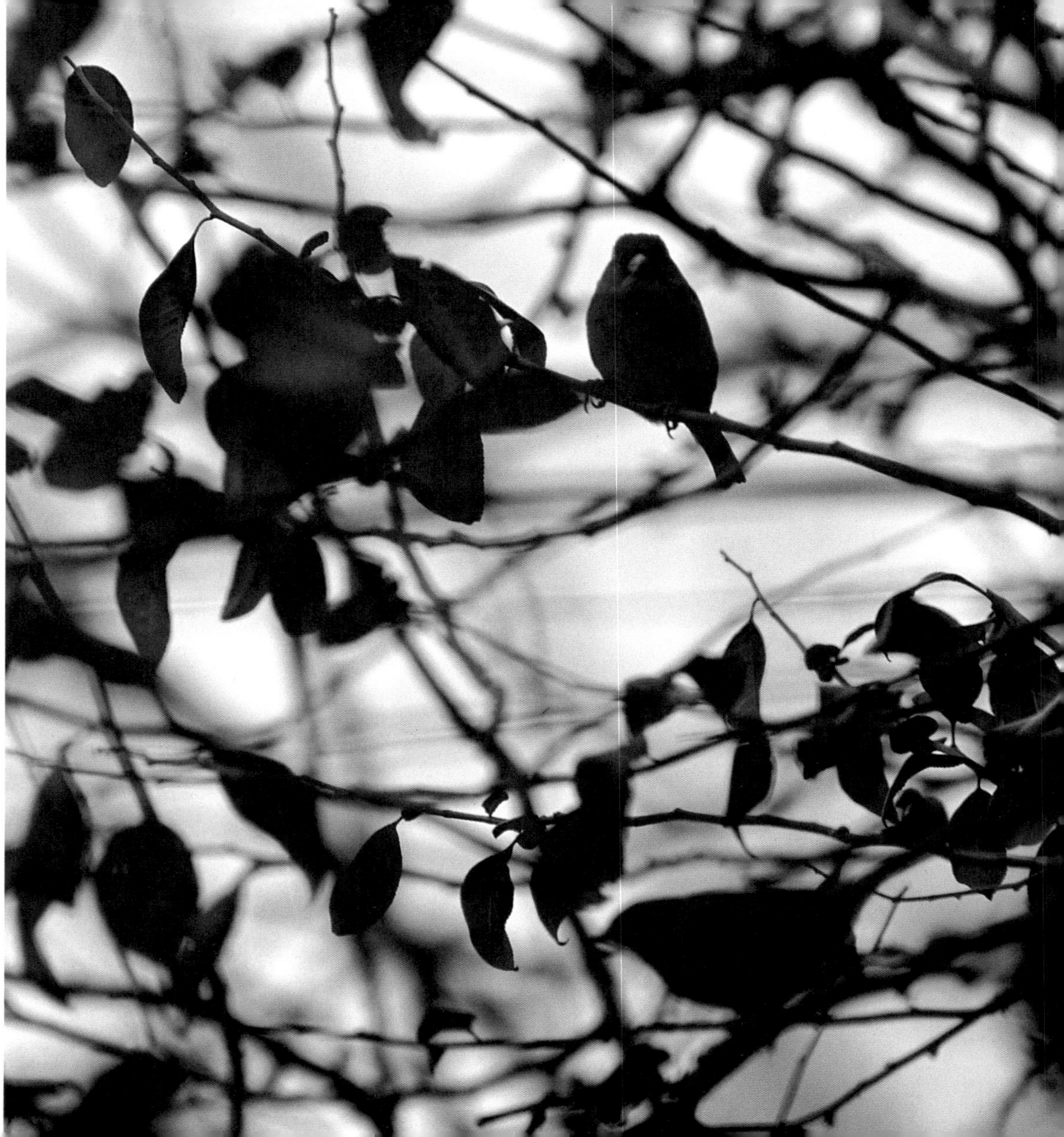

Nid untref gwadd ac eryr
The mole and the eagle do not have the same home

Nid yw gŵydd fras yn hedfan ymhell
A fat goose will not fly far

Gŵyr y cadno yn ddigon da
Pa le mae'r gwyddau yn lletya
The fox knows well enough where the geese live

Ymhell y mae llwynog yn lladd
The fox kills far from home

Nerth ysguthan yn ei hadenydd
A pigeon's strength is in its wings

Ni chân aderyn ar ei nyth
A bird will not sing on its nest

Gwingdin y llwyn, yr aderyn serchoca'n fyw
The most affectionate bird is the wagtail

Nid wrth ei big y mae prynu cyffylog
A woodcock isn't bought by looking at its beak

The wren was considered to be connected to the supernatural and on the Twelfth Night of Christmas it was caught and paraded around the neighbourhood in a box or little house, even on a small bier. This custom was acted out not only in Wales but in other countries in Europe.

Nid sionc ond y dryw
None as frisky as the wren

Neb a dynno nyth y dryw, ni chaiff iechyd yn ei fyw
He who takes the wren's nest will not with good health be blessed

40

These animals were hunted so enthusiastically that the boar and bear became extinct, with very few deer or hares left.

Nid difyrrwch ond milgi, nid digrifwch ond gwalch
No enjoyment but the hound, no amusement but the hawk

Pennaf gig hela yw carw, sgyfarnog, baedd gwyllt ac arth
The best meat of the hunt is the deer, hare, wild boar and the bear

Tri asgafaeth milgi: sgyfarnog, iwrch a llwynog
Three types of prey for a greyhound: the hare, roe-deer and fox

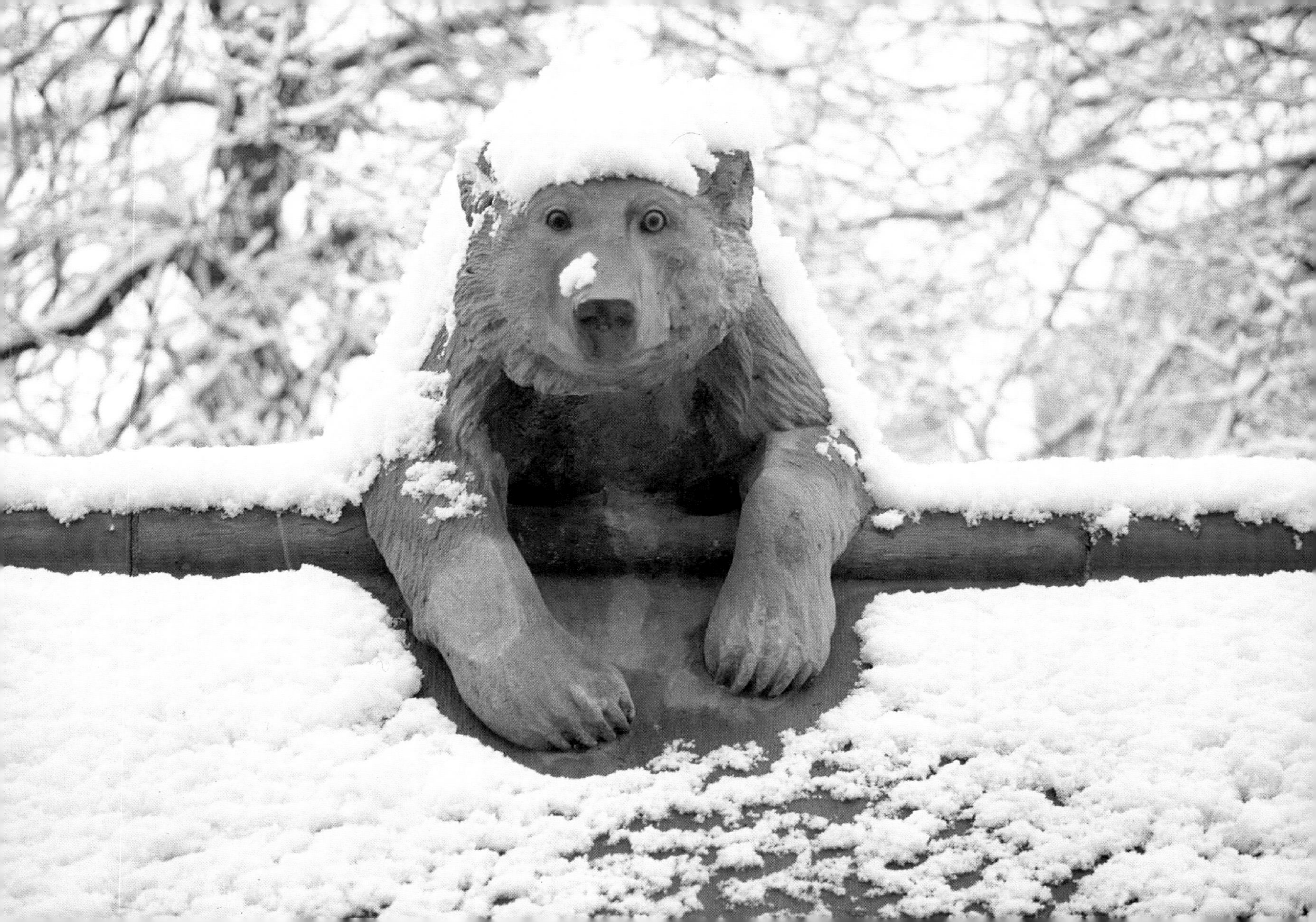

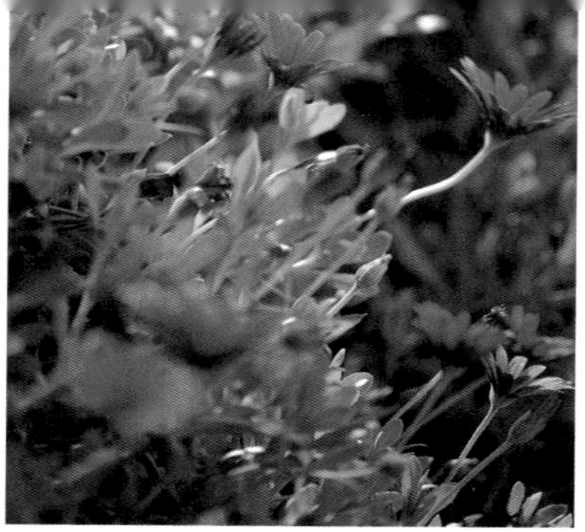

Beekeepers used to speak to their bees, telling them of important events in the family. Whilst modern beekeepers do not admit to going to such depth in their one-way conversations, they do happily admit to speaking to their bees now and again.

Gorau llwyddiant, gwenyn
Bees are most successful

Er heddwch nac er rhyfel, gwenyn farw ni chasgl fêl
Neither in war or peace will a dead bee gather honey

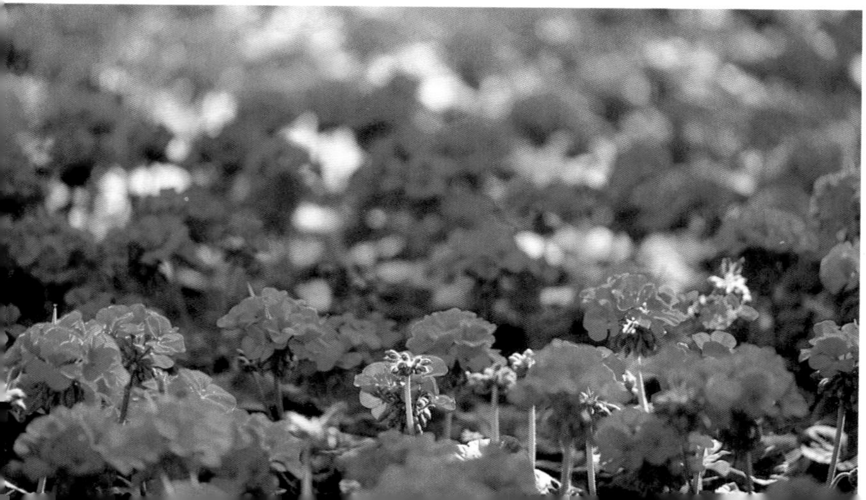

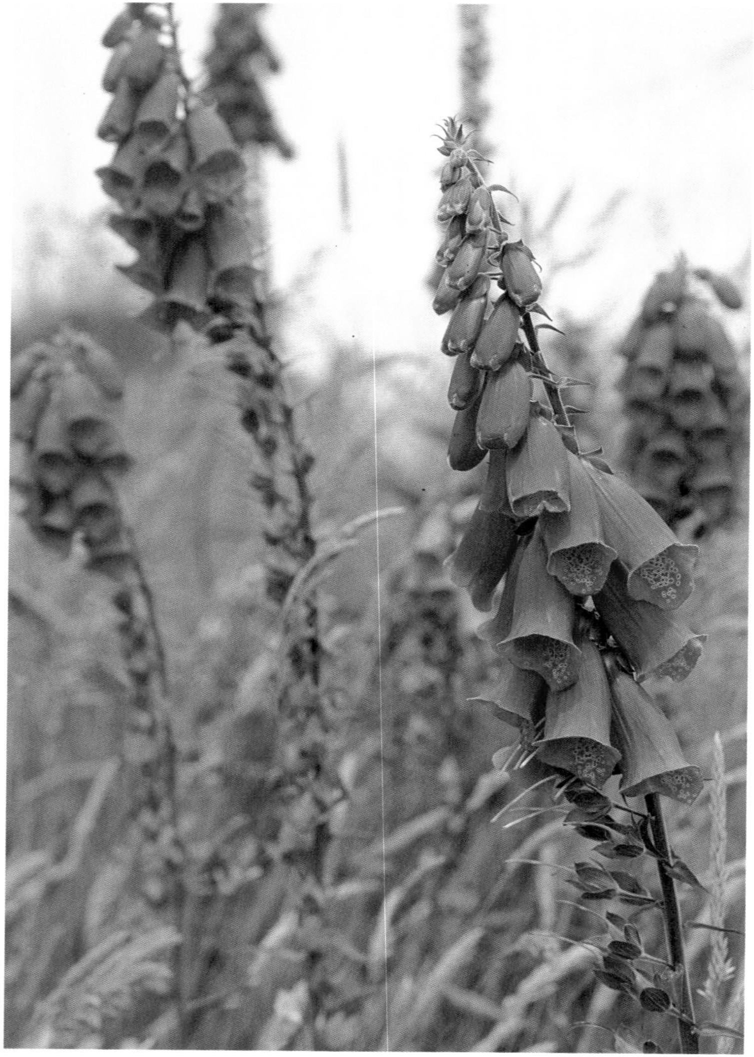

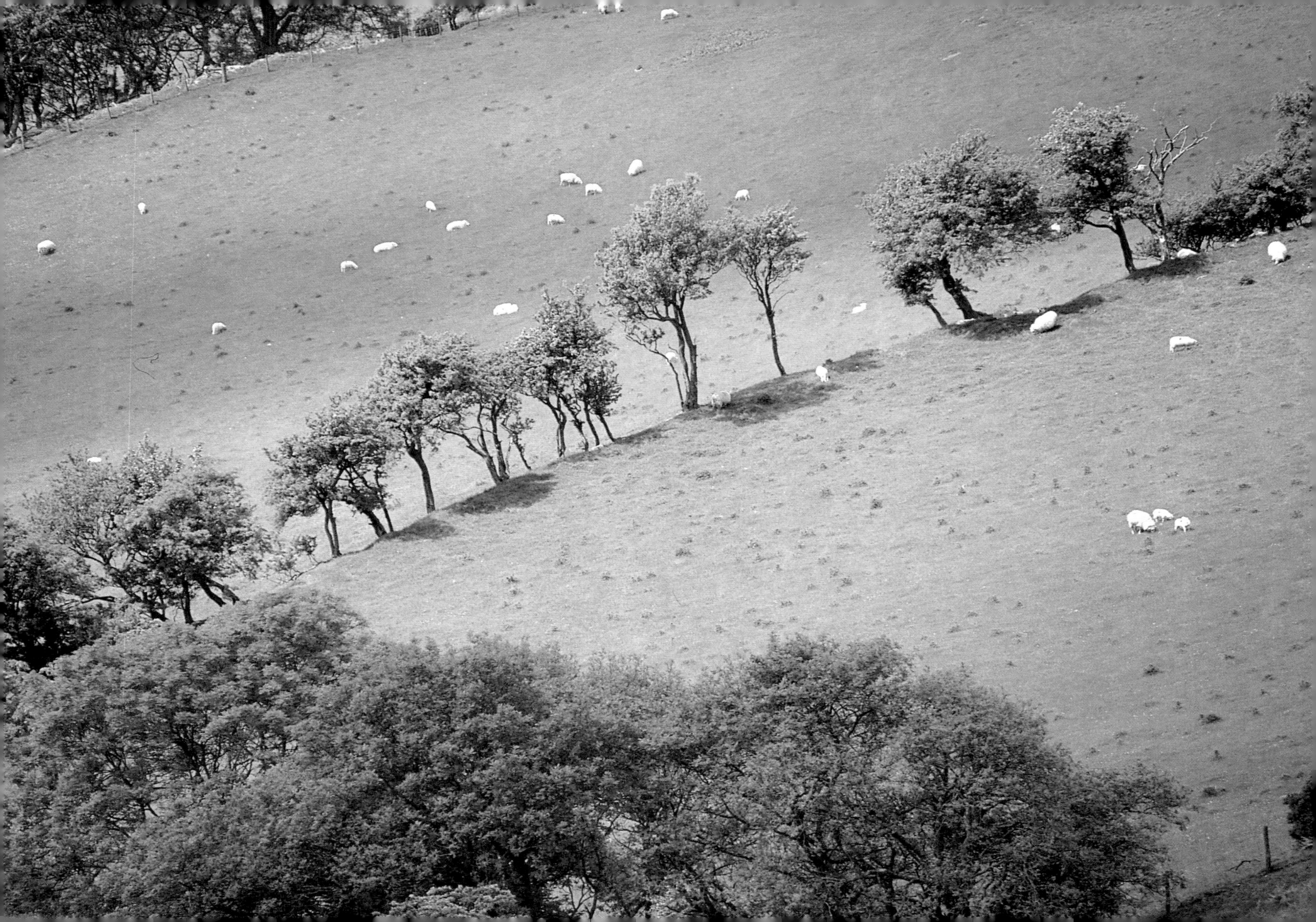

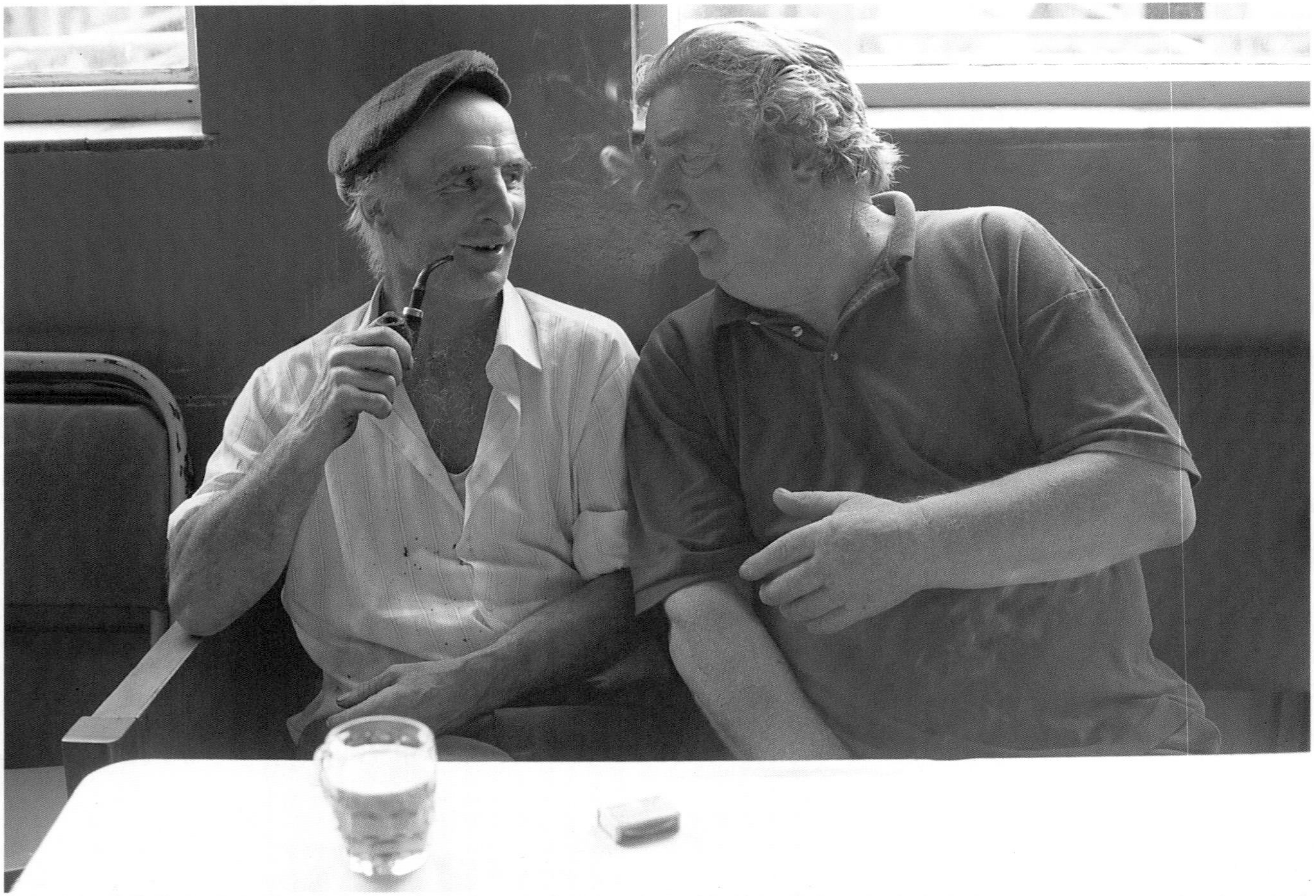

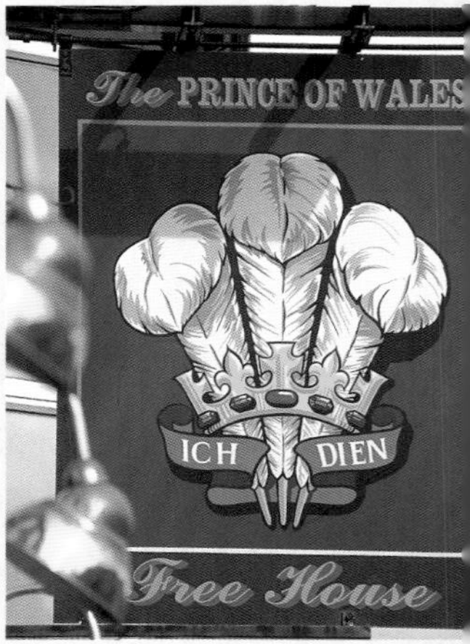
The PRINCE OF WALES
ICH DIEN
Free House

One of the Celts' greatest weaknesses was, and is, their fondness for strong drink! The Romans had not drunk beer until they came into contact with the Celts and they took the Celtic word for it ('corma') into their own language; today it is still 'cerveza' in Spanish and cwrw in Welsh. Similarly the Celtic aristocracy took a rapid liking to the wine ofthe Romans, and archaeological evidence from Dinas Powis reveals that wines from the Mediterranean continued to be imported into Wales long after the departure of the legionaries.

Mead, a strong alcoholic drink made from honey, was also prized by the Celts and in Welsh the word for getting drunk is still meddwi - to get 'meaded'. In the area around Caerleon there is a story that when the Romans arrived in the region they came up against a tribe called The Silures - people they said could not be subdued by kindness or cruelty. When the legion had been there for a long period without strong drink, a group of soldiers were sent out to take captives, so that they could obtain the secret of making mead.

The soldiers eventually captured an old man and his son, and demanded the secret. The old man replied that he would tell them the secret if they killed his son, because he had done him many wrongs. The thirsty Romans quickly carried out his wishes, but the old man looked at them with disdain and said,"My son was weak and would have given you the secret anyway, but now you can kill me too, because you will never get it from me."

True or not, the story demonstrates the Celts' passion for drink and their stubborn resistance to the Romans.

In the late eighteenth and nineteenth centuries, when parts of Wales experienced rapid industrialisation and urbanisation, alcohol, and beer in particular, was very popular with the working classes-probably to help them forget the harshness of their living and working conditions. Until it was outlawed, children as young as four worked underground in the iron ore and coal mines and were early recruits for alcohol and tobacco. The temperance movement developed as an antidote to the excesses of the period, and landowners like Lady Llanover bought up taverns and turned them into temperance houses.

45

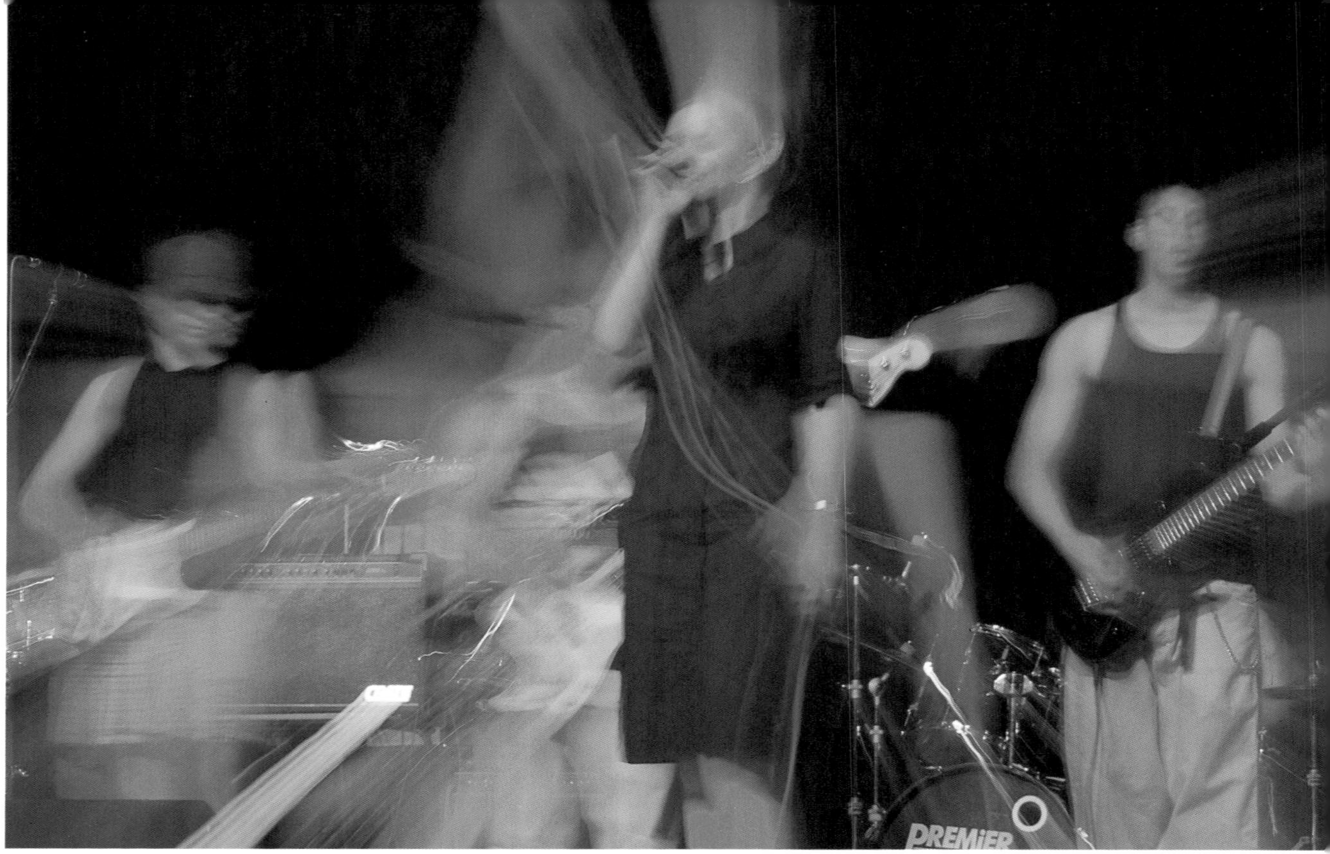
PREMiER

Tabler i lysiau, tafarn i chwedlau
The sideboard for vegetables, the tavern for stories

Allwedd calon, cwrw da
Good ale is the key to the heart

Segurdod a meddwdod a wna grogyddion yn gyfoethog
Idleness and drunkeness keep hangmen rich

Medd a ddiosg y mwgwd
Mead will take off the mask

Chweg medd pan yfer; chwerw pan daler
Mead is sweet when drunk but bitter when paid for

Gwin yn y bol, twrw yn y pen
Wine in the belly, a tumult in the head

AMSER, IEUENCTID A HENAINT/ TIME, YOUTH AND OLD AGE

In the past, birth, ageing and death were much more immediate experiences than they are today, where everything can seem neatly compartmentalised and distanced - women give birth in hospitals, children are sent off to schools, the elderly move into old people's homes and often die amongst strangers. There was a time when growing old brought respect for accumulated wisdom, but today this knowledge is not considered to be of great value.

Of course, living in close proximity to each other, as everyone did until quite recently, would have had disadvantages as well as benefits, but one suspects that the various age groups gained much greater understanding of each other simply because they had greater daily contact.

Ni ddaw doe byth
Yesterday never returns

Hen a ŵyr, ifanc a dybia
The old know, the young surmise

Llwyd pob hen
All the old are grey

Ni cheir gwaith gŵr gan was
A man's work is not obtained from a boy

Nid ffŵl fel hen ffŵl
No fool like an old fool

'*Rhag angau ni thycia ffo*
From death there is no escape

Nid cyngor ond tad, nid gweddi ond mam
No counsel but a father's, no prayer but a mother's

Unwaith yn ddyn, dwywaith yn blentyn
Once a man, twice a child

Amser a dangnofa bob hiraeth
Time soothes all longing

Llaeth i blentyn, cig i'r gŵr, cwrw i hen
Milk for a child, meat for a man, and beer for the old

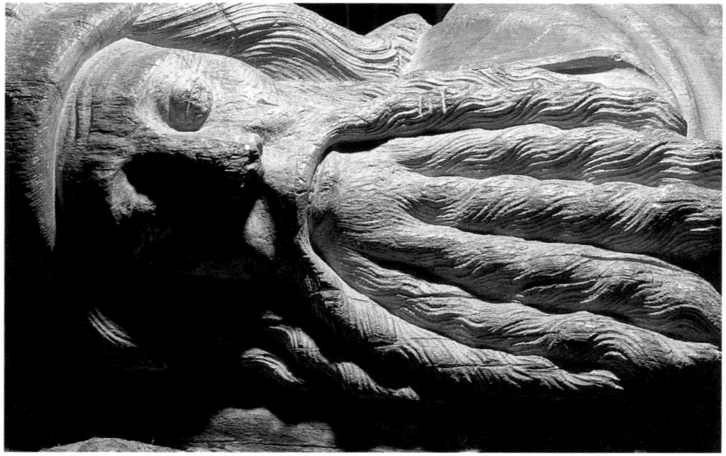

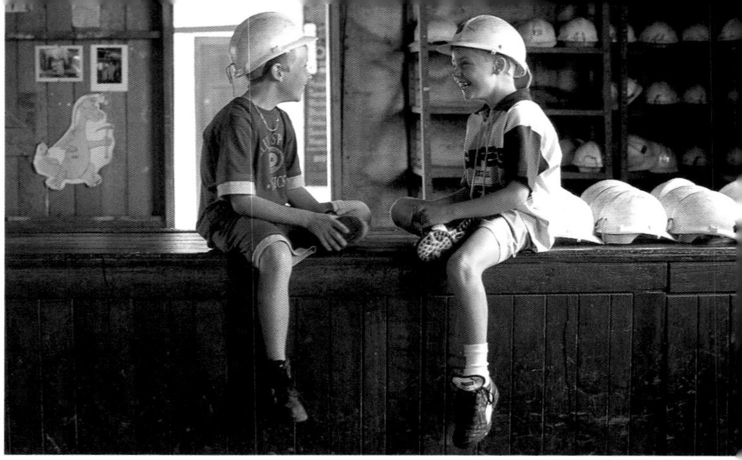

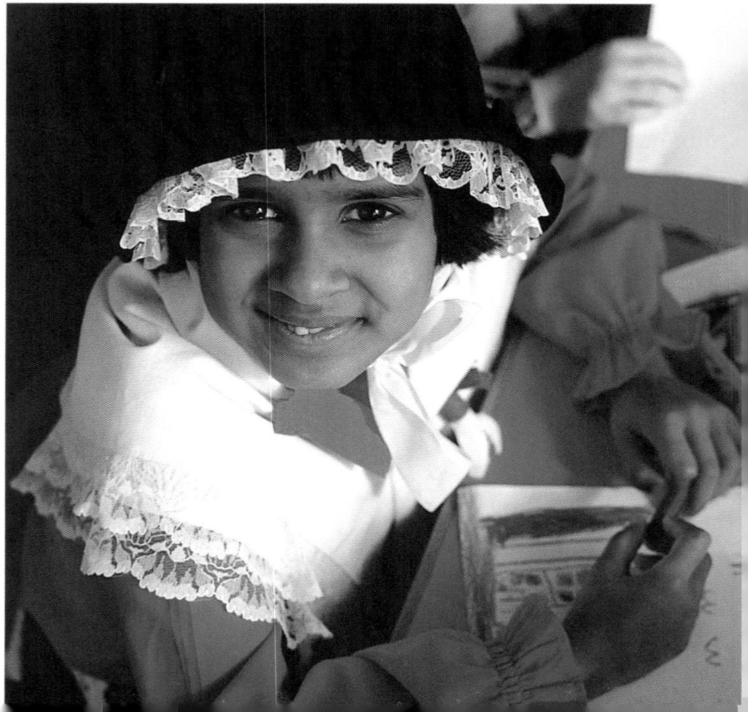

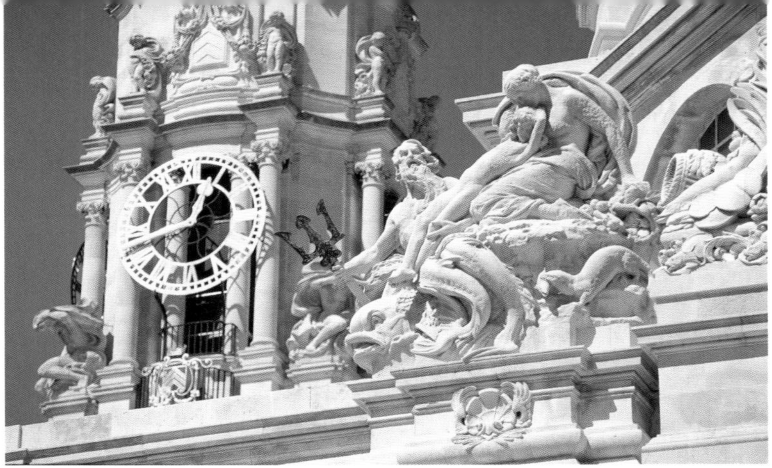

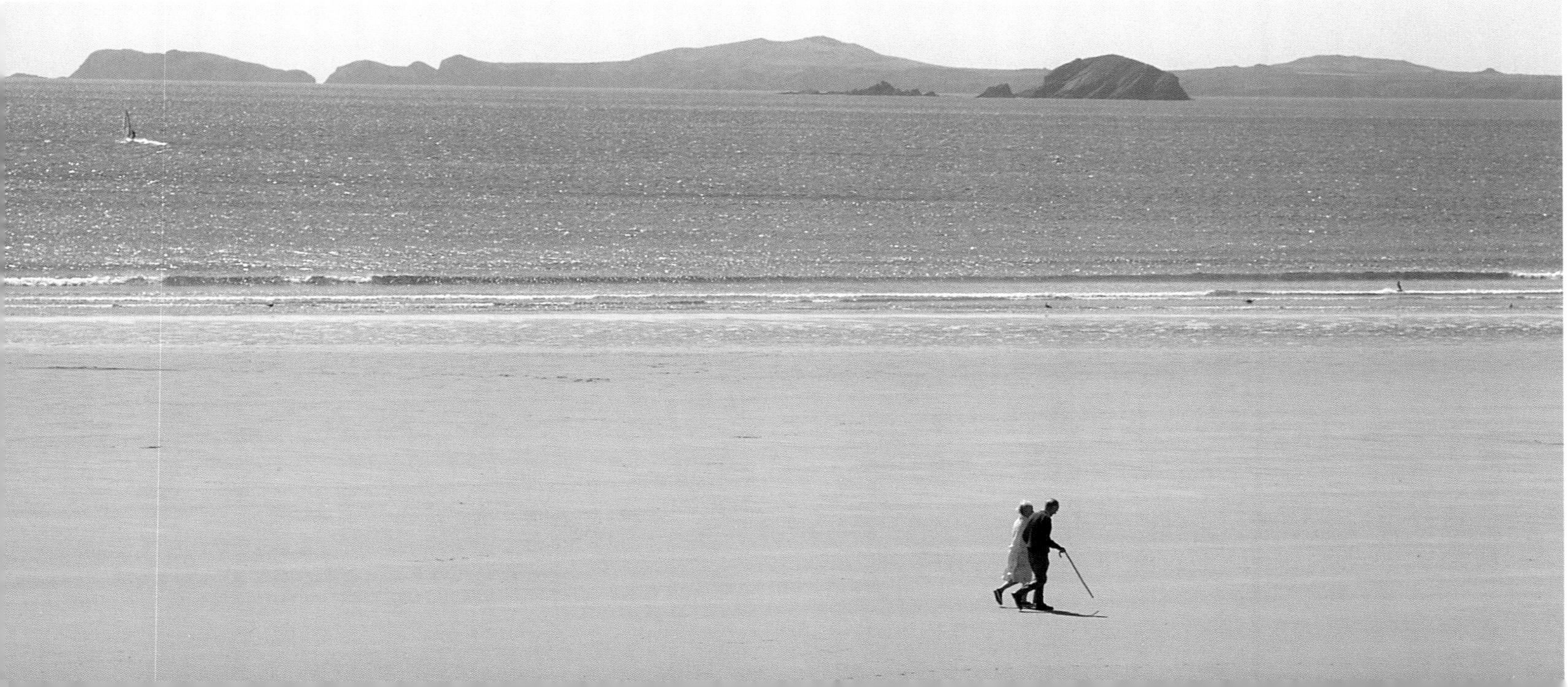

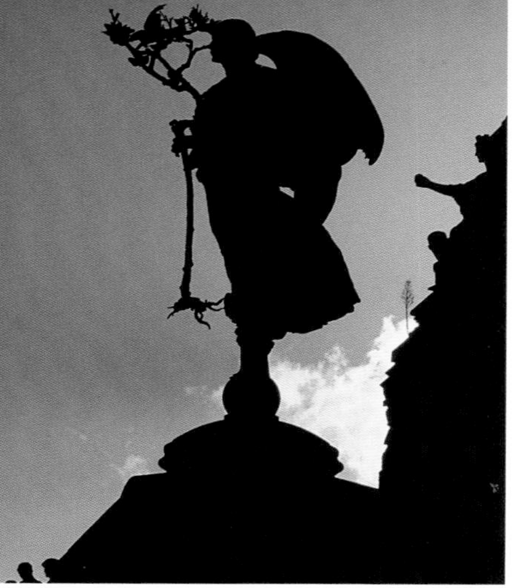

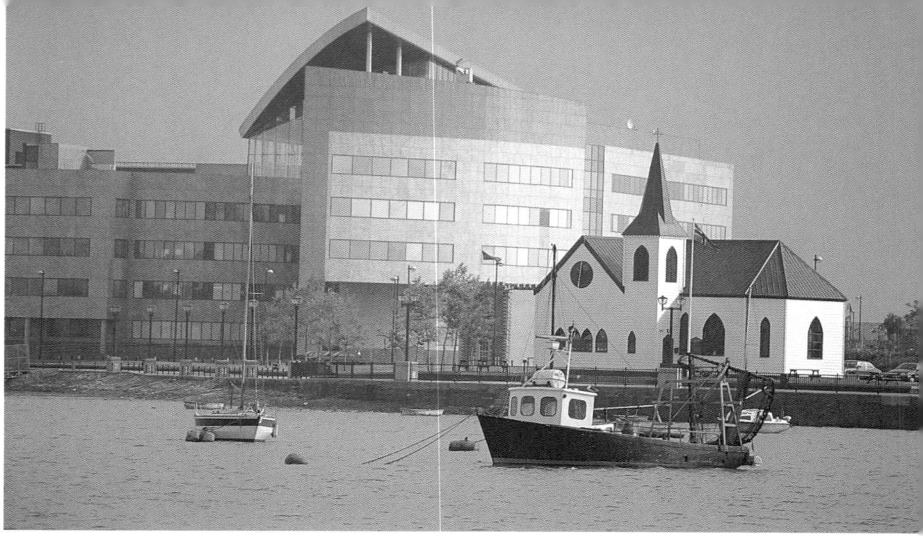

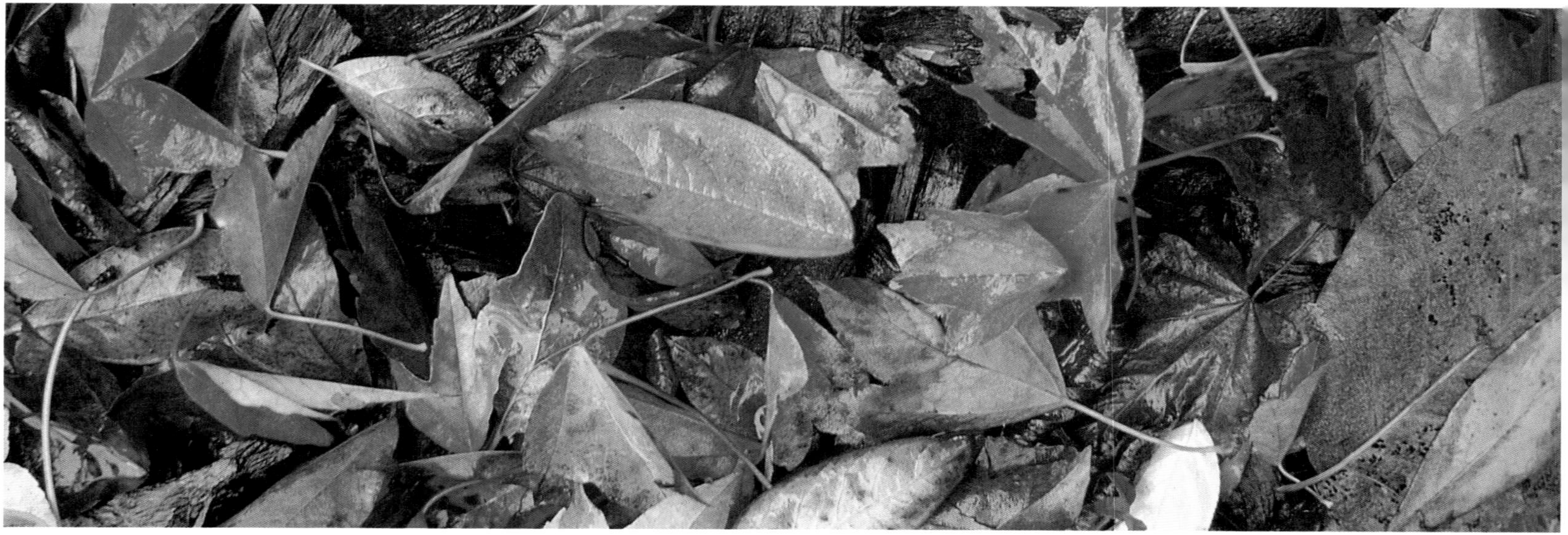

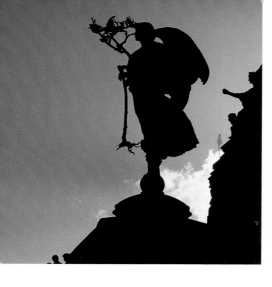

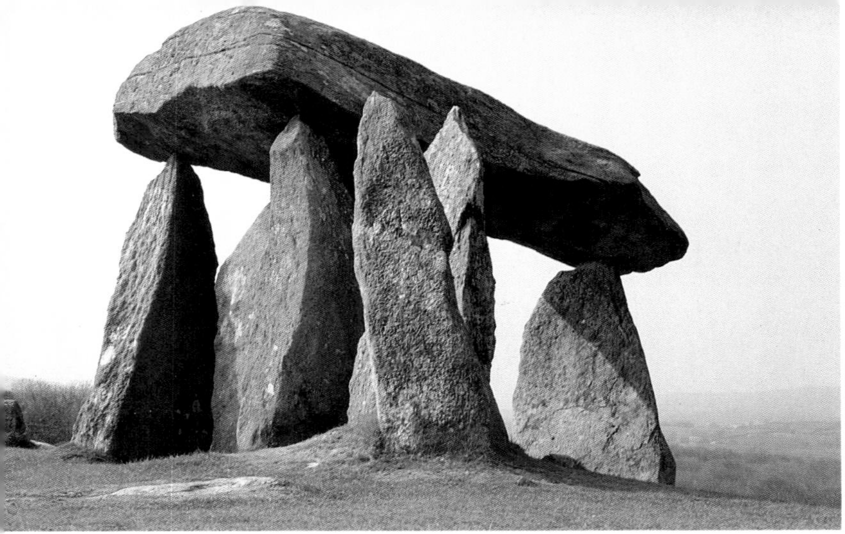

Bûm gall unwaith - hynny oedd, llefain pan ym ganed
I was wise once - I cried when I was born

Ni edrych angau pwy decaf ei dalcen
Death does not consider who is fairest of forehead

Chwiban i faban, aradr i'r gŵr
A whistle for a child, a plough for a man

O bob trwm, trymaf henaint
Of all weights the heaviest is old age

Tri chysur henaint: tân, te a tybaco
The three comforts of old age: fire, tea and tobacco

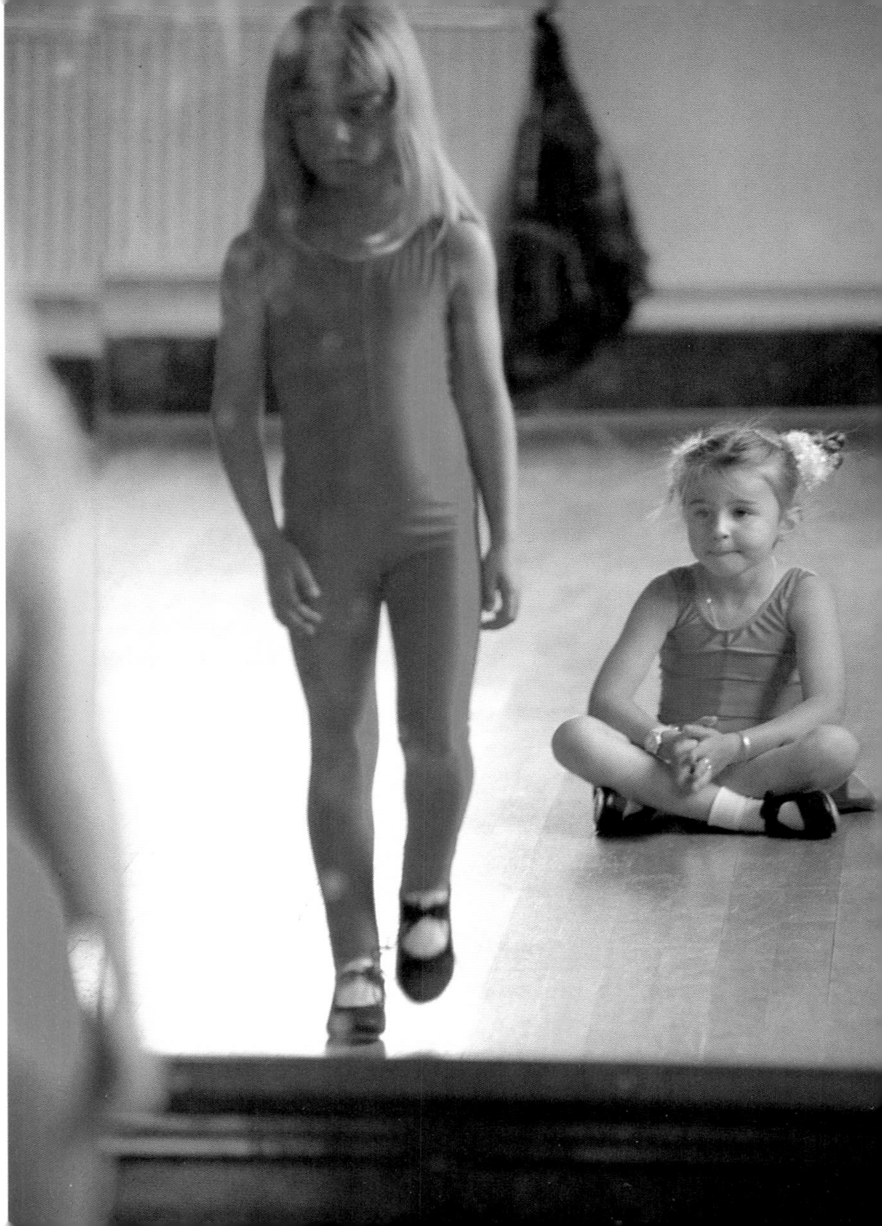

IECHYD / HEALTH

One of the best ways of avoiding illness has always been by healthy living; trial and error over hundreds of years has led people to know what is good and bad for them.

In the sixteenth century the use of herbs was important in curing ailments and perhaps the most famous herbalists in the whole of Britain were the Physicians of Myddfai, a family who had their origins in the small village of Myddfai near Carmarthen in south Wales. Their accumulated body of knowledge was finally written down by John Pughe in 1861 - nearly twenty years after the death of the last known surviving member of the family, Dr. Rice Williams of Aberystwyth.

A fynno iechyd, bid lawen
If you desire health, be happy

Tri enllyn iechyd - mêl, menyn a llaeth
Three of health's sauces - honey, butter and milk

Tri enllyn afiechyd - cig, cwrw ac aesel
Three of sickness's sauces - meat, beer and vinegar

Nid meddyg ond amser
Time is the only doctor

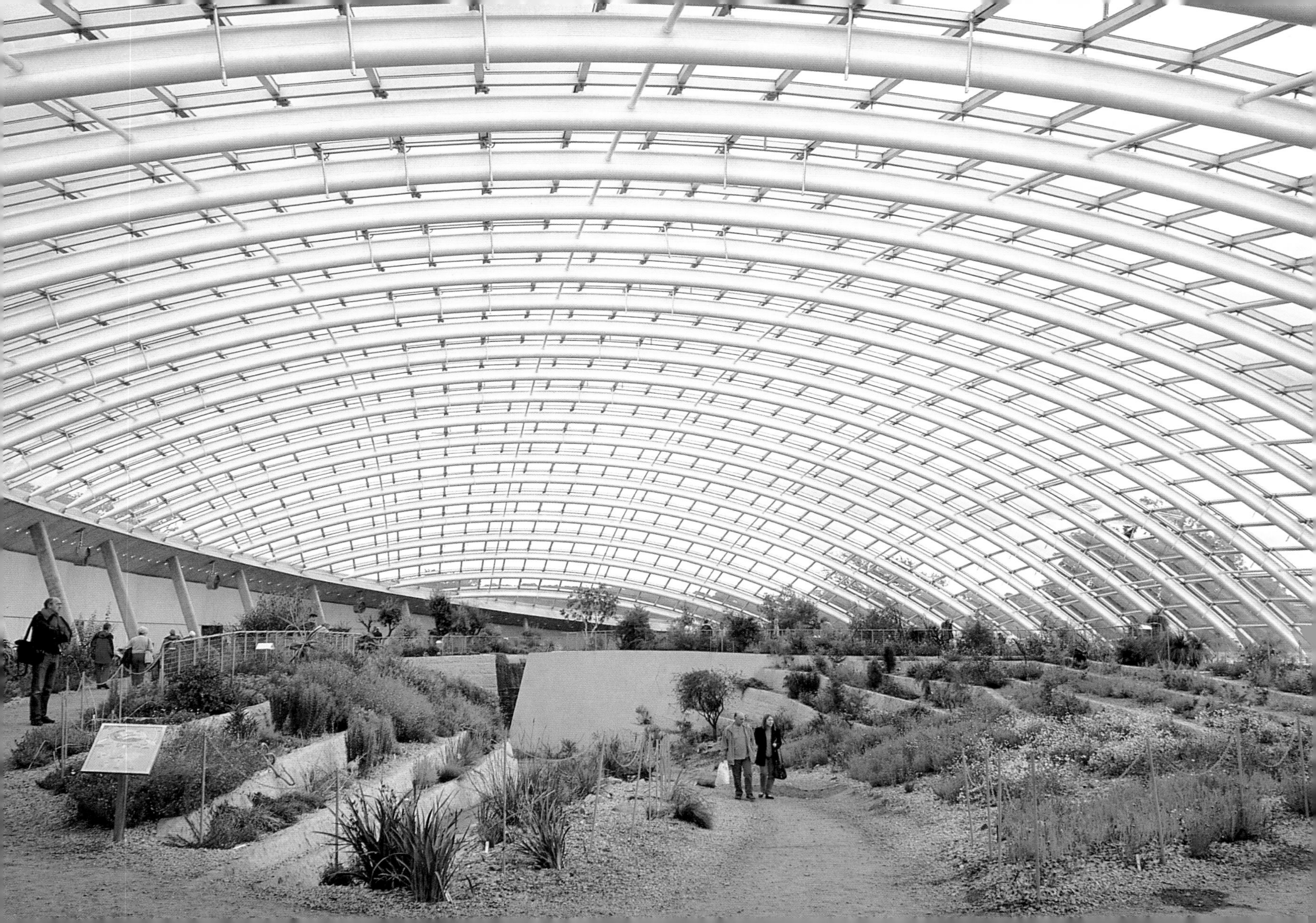

Nid meddyg fel cyfaill
No doctor like a friend

Nid oes meddyg rhag henaint
No doctor can ward off old age

Bara ddoe, cig heddiw a gwin llynedd a bair iechyd
Yesterday's bread, today's meat and last year's wine will bring health

Tri dyn a fyddant hiroesog - aradwr sychdir, hafodwr mynydd a physgotwr môr
Three men that live long - a ploughman of dry land, a mountain farmer and a sea fisherman

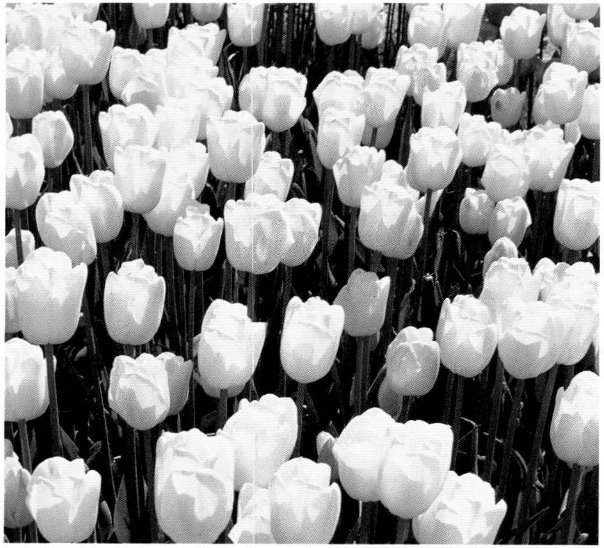

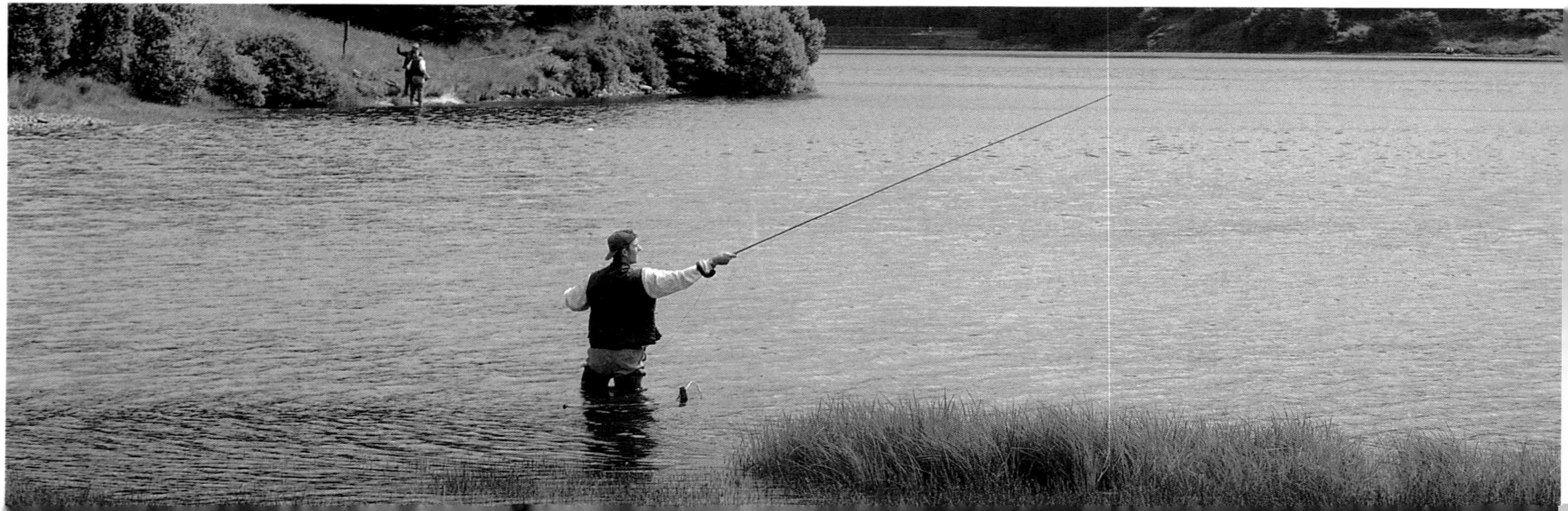

Y FELIN / THE MILL

When bread was the staple diet of the majority of people in Europe, before the advent of the potato, the mill was one of the most important buildings in any community. If grain was not taken to the mill, it would be practically impossible to make it into flour. Of course, hand querns were an alternative, but unless there was a team of slaves, as in Ancient Egypt, the process of hand milling was too time consuming to contemplate.

When water mills were at their peak there were literally thousands along the rivers of Wales; today there are fewer than a dozen working water mills and only one working windmill, so their importance is now difficult for us to imagine.

The miller was open to many accusations: the most common was that of stealing grain, because normally it was left and collected later. Once it was ground into flour it was difficult to be sure of exact amounts.

It was natural enough for people to chat with the miller when they brought the grain to the mill, so he was also considered to be a good source of gossip.

Tri thlws cenedl - melin, cored a pherllan
A nation's three jewels are its mill, weir and orchard

Cyntaf i'r felin a gaiff falu
The first to the mill shall grind

Chwedlau'r gwragedd yn y felin
Stories of the women in the mill

Gwneud melin ac eglwys ohoni
To make a mill and church of it i.e. To make a mountain out of a molehill

Mae'r melinydd yn dwyn beichiau eraill
The miller takes on the burdens of others

Caffad malu, caffad ei werth
Grain taken for grinding must be paid for

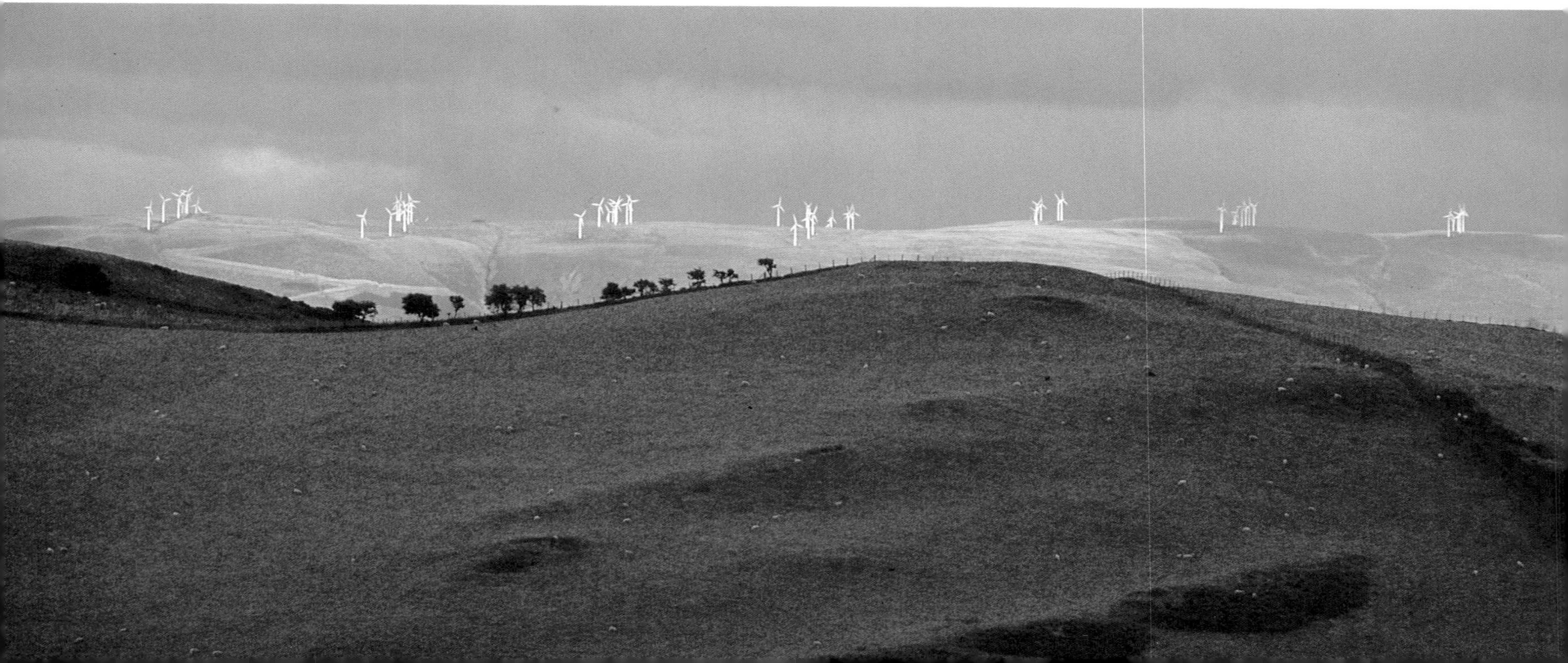

BWYD / FOOD

Just as in the other Celtic countries, the griddle, or bakestone as it is also called, has long been an important utensil for cooking on. Welsh cakes (pice ar y maen) are still baked on them, as are pancakes (crempog), together with various types of bread. Our cawl, a broth that uses meats like salt beef, mutton and pork, together with any available vegetables, is related to the Galician soup called caldo. In the past, however, as the proverbs show, hunger was never far from the thoughts of the average man and woman.

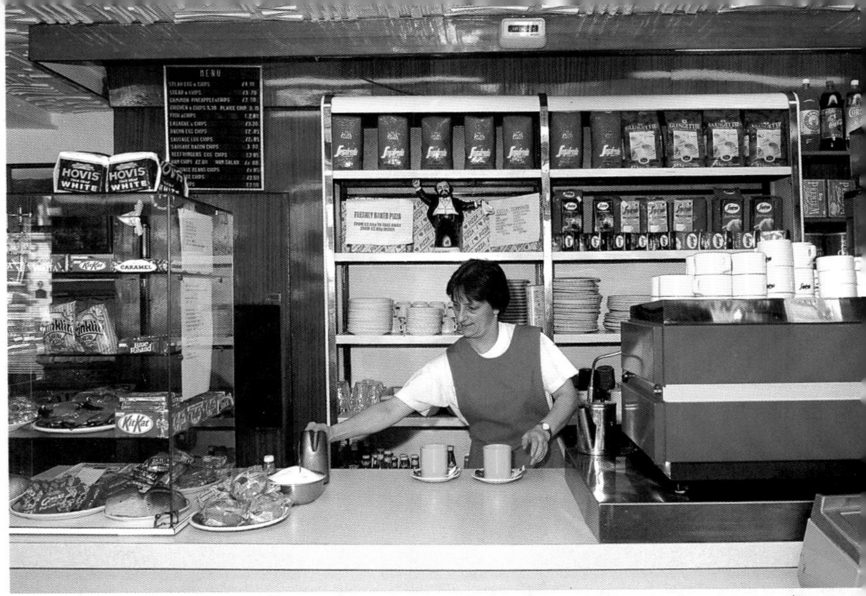
HOVIS WHITE
HOVIS WHITE
CARAMEL

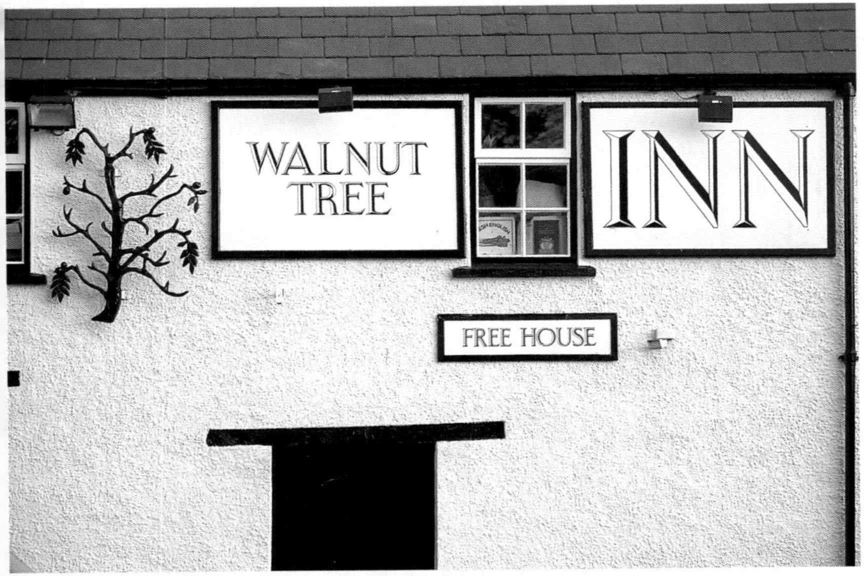
WALNUT TREE
INN
FREE HOUSE

Na fwyta ond i dorri newyn
Do not eat except to satisfy hunger

Yf ddŵr fel ych a gwin fel brenin
Drink water like an ox and wine like a king

Cynildeb yw un wŷ, boneddigeiddrwydd yw dau, glewder yw tri a dihirdra yw'r pedwerydd
One egg is economy, two is gentility, three is greed and four is wickedness

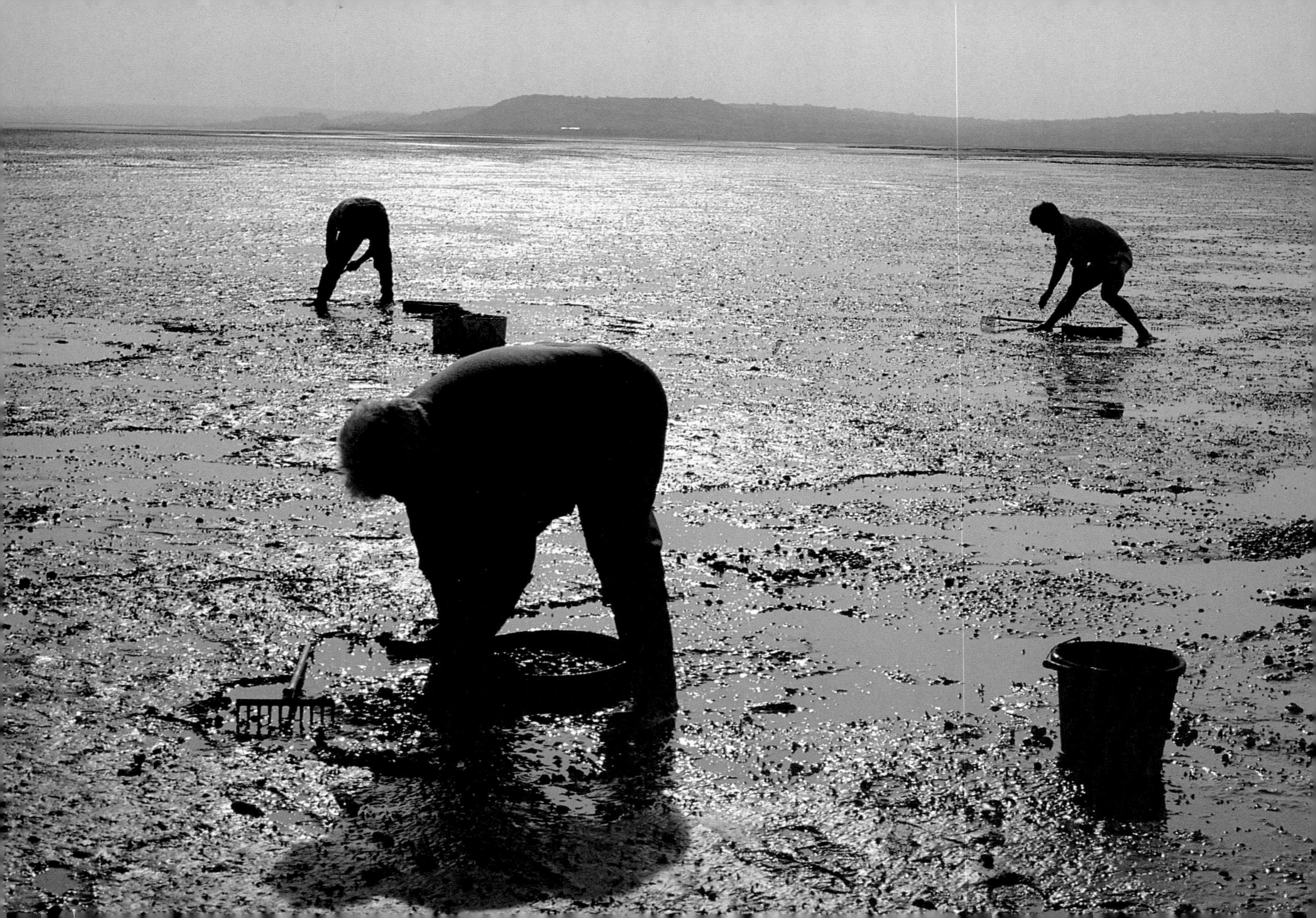

Mwstard wedi bwyd
Mustard after food

Mynn mis, oen tri mis
A kid a month old, a lamb three months old

Caws defaid, llaeth geifr a menyn gwartheg sydd orau
Cheese from sheep, milk from a goat and butter from cattle are best

Dau bryd newynog a wna'r trydydd yn lwth
Two hungry meals make the third gluttonous

Malltan tân uwd, mellten tân lymru
A slow fire under porridge, lightning under flummery

Ffon y bywyd yw bara
Bread is the staff of life

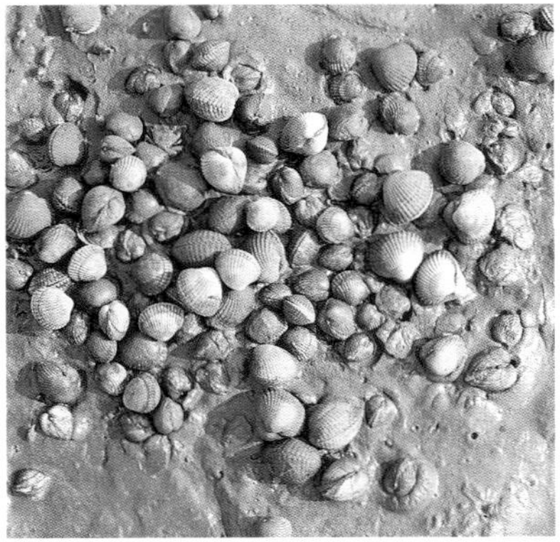

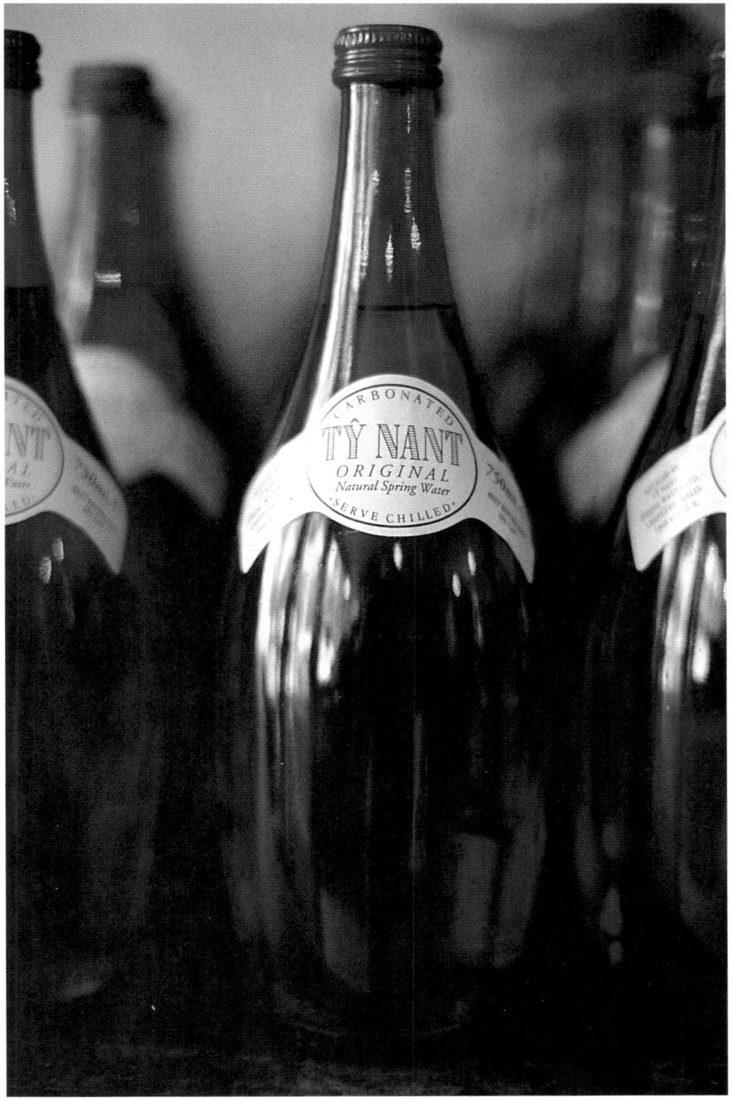
CARBONATED
TŶ NANT
ORIGINAL
Natural Spring Water
SERVE CHILLED

Until relatively recently, only the gentry and their entourage had the time and money for entertainment of any kind, and it is generally forgotten that, for the masses, attending religious services was in some ways a popular form of entertainment, with communal singing and stiring sermons.

In Wales, however, entertainment for the gentry was amongst the most sophisticated in Europe, owing much to the long bardic traditions. The poetry was so well crafted that it can still be favourably compared with most English poetry of the period. Even today, Welsh poets compete with each other on the radio every week - something that would probably be unthinkable in any other language.

The music, which is only now being properly interpreted, is courtly and considerably removed from folk music. As far as we know, most poetry was originally sung to music, which made it more entertaining for the listener and also easier for the performer to remember.

The Welsh harp was played in a different way from today, using the nails, then damping the strings with the tips of the fingers. The crwth was superseded by the fiddle, although it was quite a different instrument and played in a different way. The pibgorn or hornpipe makes truly electrifying music, which is now gradually being played once more.

Ni waeth beth fo lliw'r delyn os da'r gainc
The harp's colour doesn't matter as long as the tune is good

Tair cynneddf telynor: peri chwerthin, llefain a chysgu
The three qualities of a harpist: to cause laughter, tears and slumber

Digon o grwth a thelyn
Plenty of crwth and harp (meaning that a person has had enough)

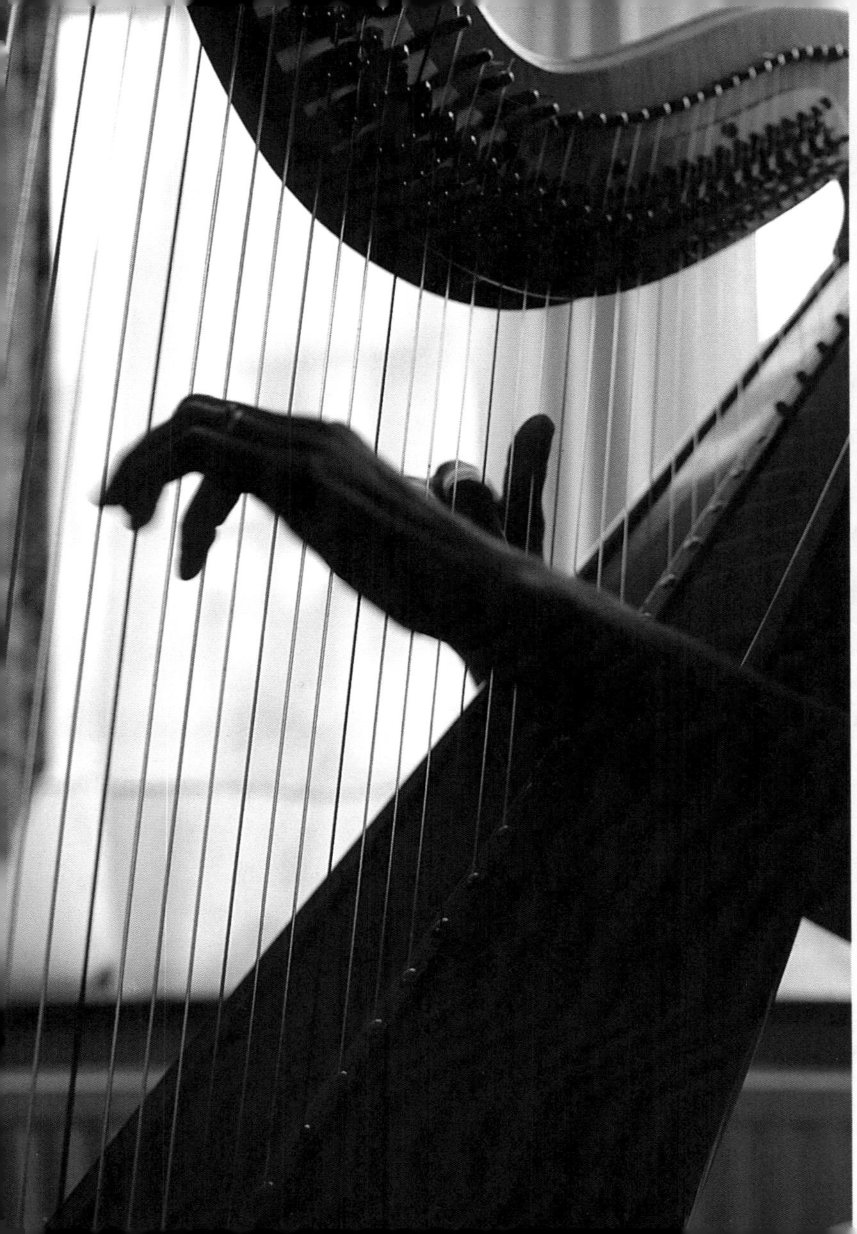

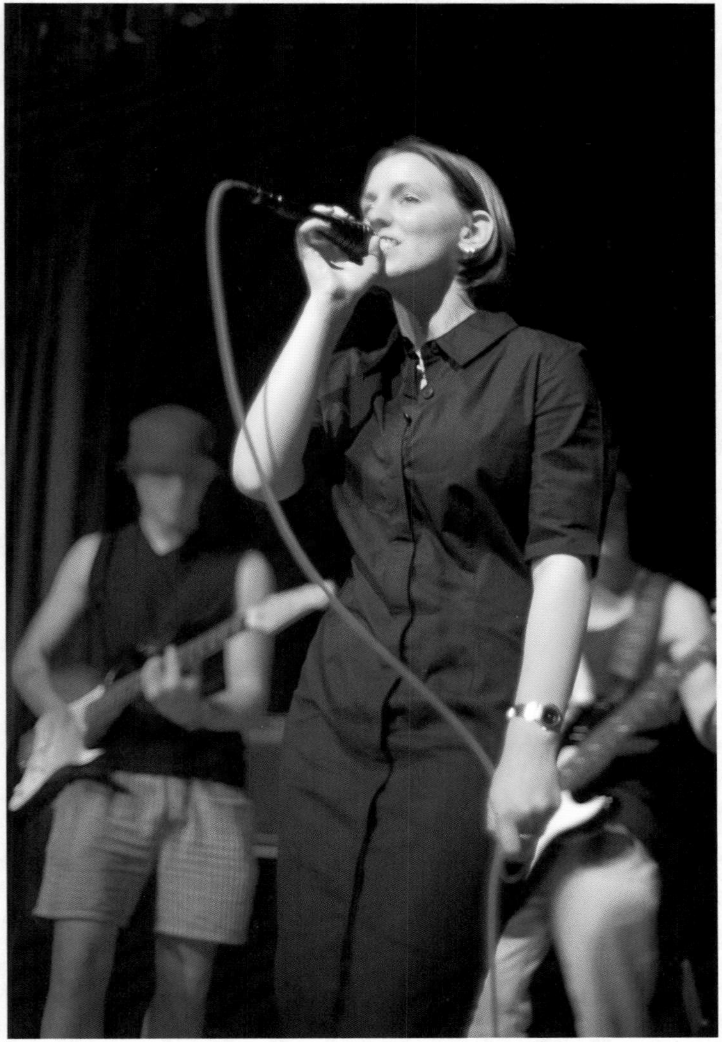

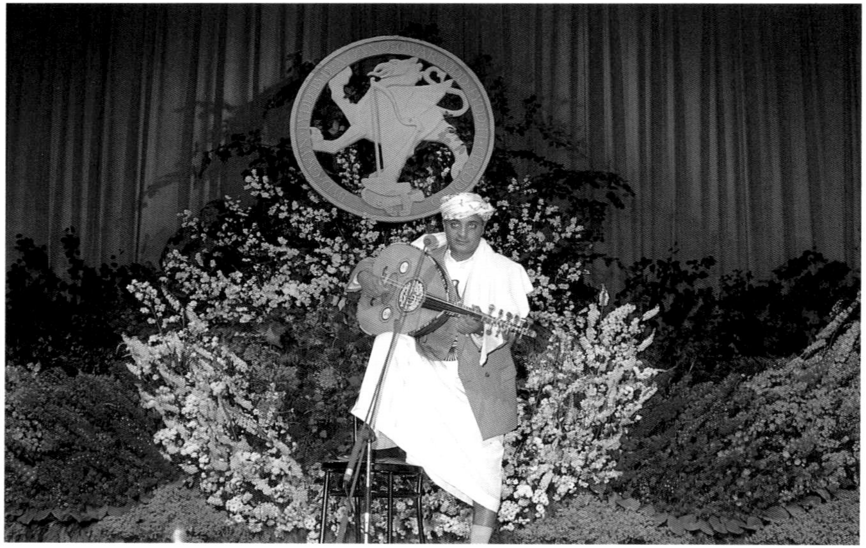

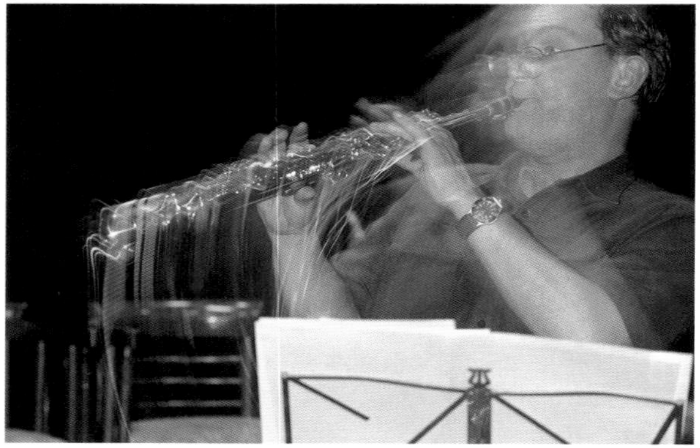

Diwedd y gân yw'r geiniog
The end of the song is the penny

A gorelwo, taled i'r crythor
Let him who dances pay the fiddler
(the man who plays the crwth)

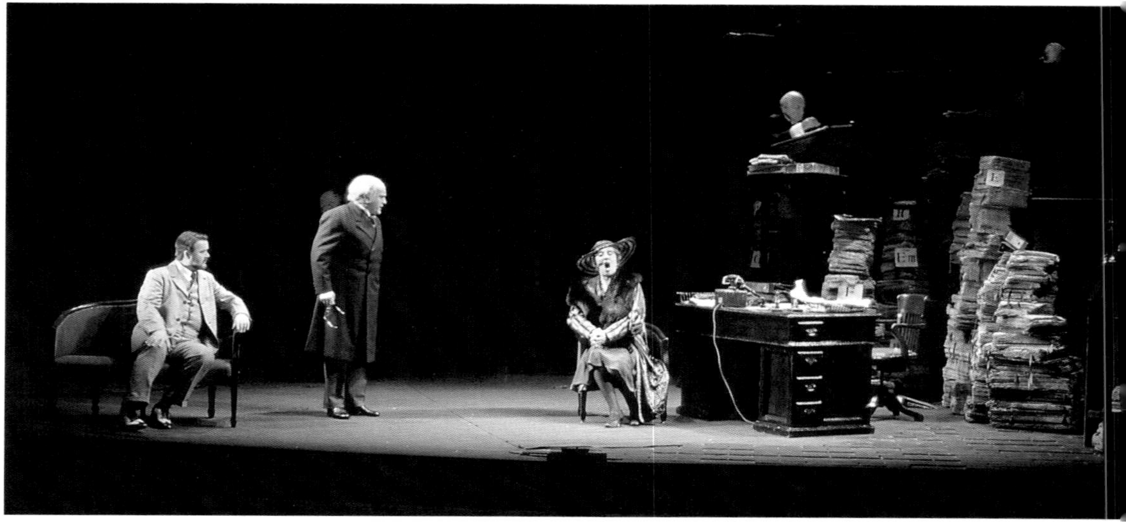

GWAITH A CHREFFT / WORK AND CRAFT

Crafts have a long tradition in Wales and the Celtic world in general. One of the most venerated craftsmen was the blacksmith, whose ability to transform dull iron into shining tools and weapons lent him a mystical quality, and in Wales the smith-god was known as Gofannon. There are theories that many of the patterns on Celtic objects had magical symbolism, which would also have lent the maker an air of the supernatural.

On a more mundane level, craftsmen were required to create objects that were primarily useful and, if possible, attractive as well. But for craftsman and ordinary worker alike, the day was long and hard, with little recompense.

Tri dyn a wna gyfannedd lle bônt: bardd, gof a thelynor
Three men who make an abode wherever they may be: a bard, a smith and a harpist

Nid oes neb mor droednoeth â phlant y crydd
There are none as bare-footed as the cobbler's children

Gwell crefft na golud
Better a craft than wealth

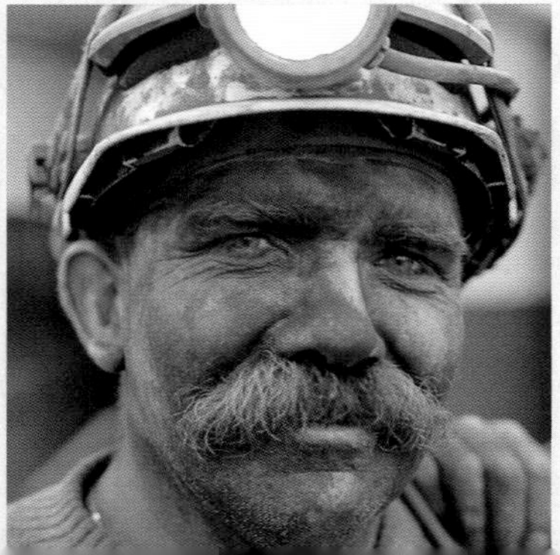

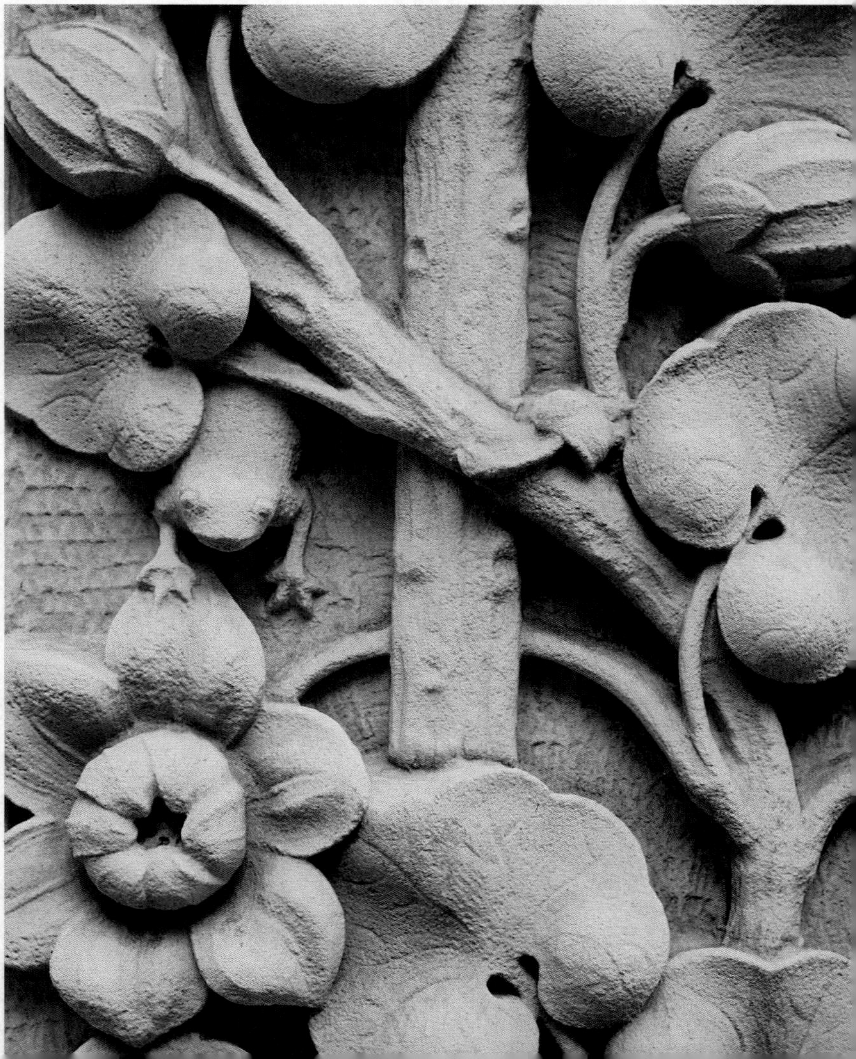

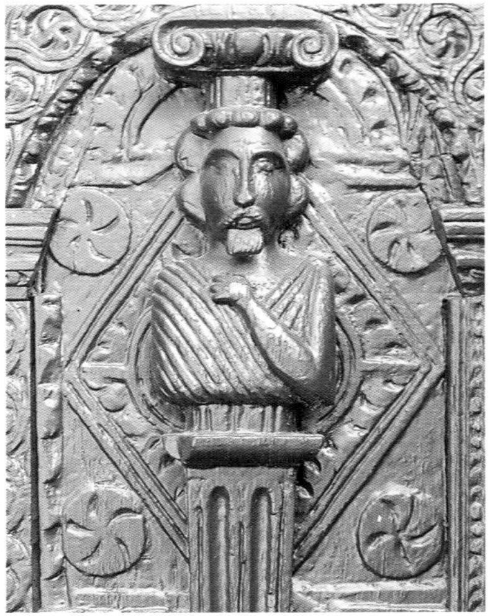

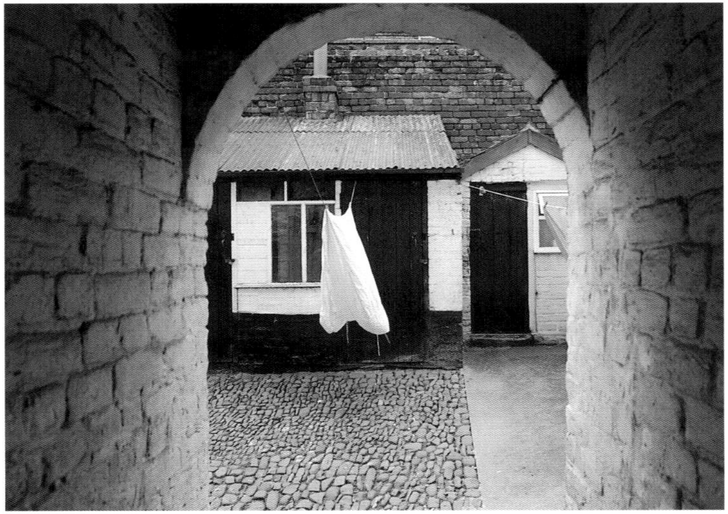

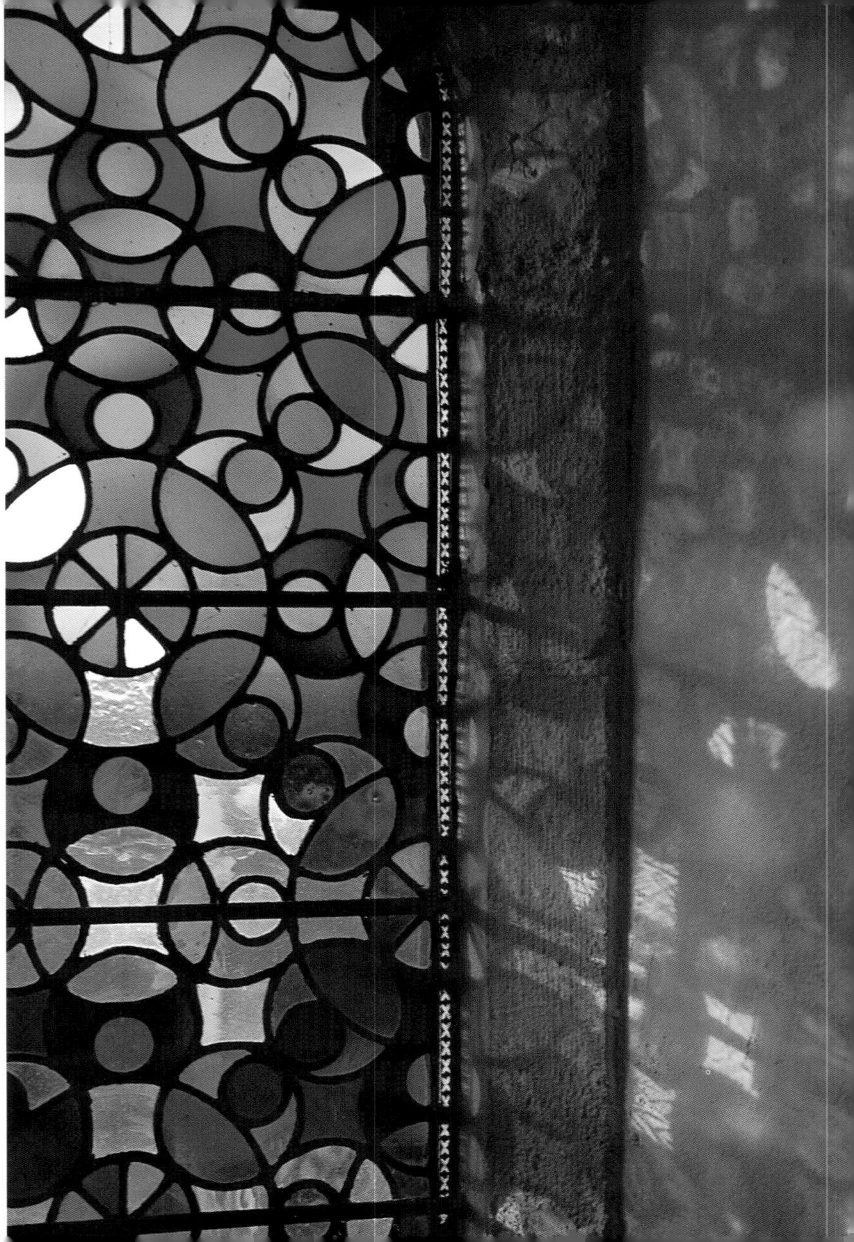

‘*Arfer yw hanner y gwaith*
Practice is half the work

Cyn dechrau gwêl y diwedd
Before starting consider the end

Llaw frys, llaw gywrain
The swift hand is the skilled hand

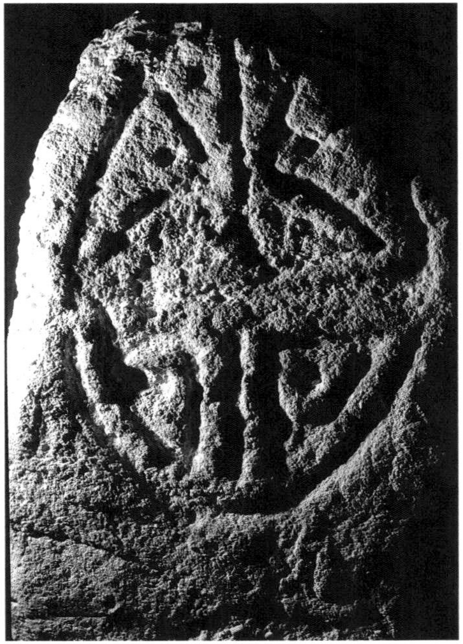

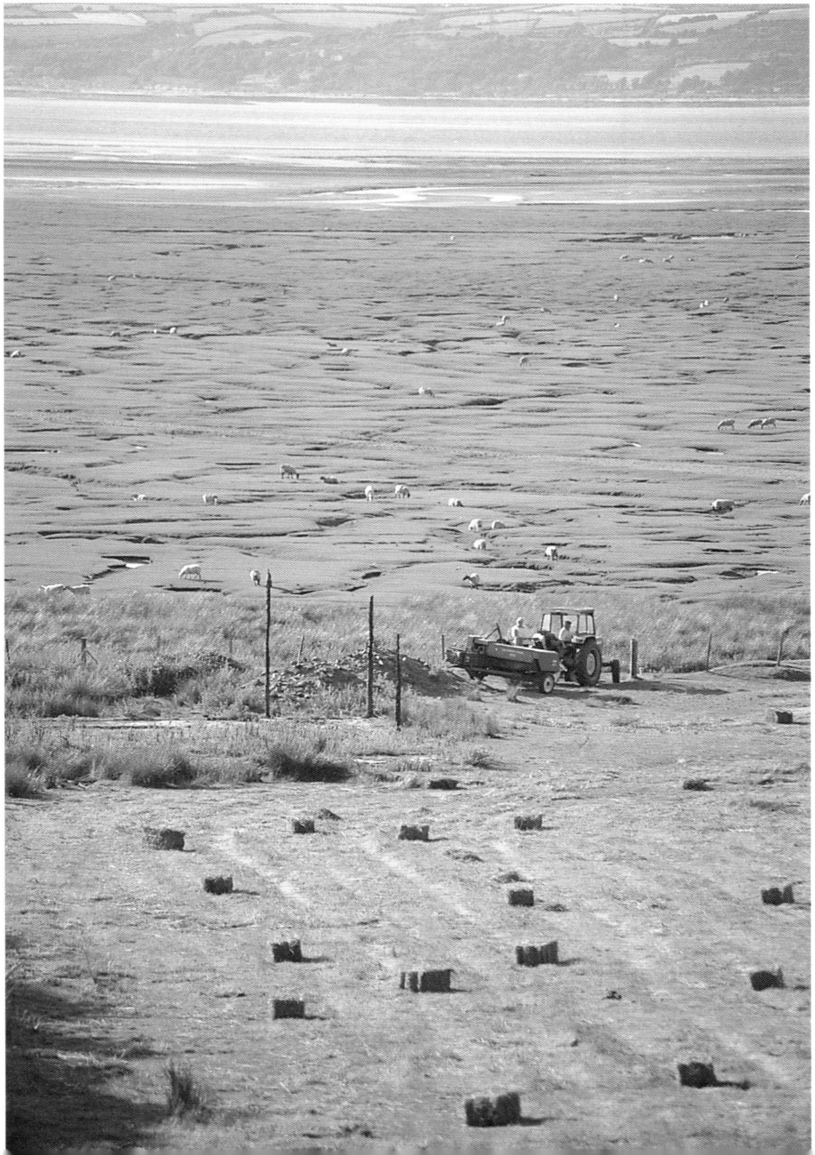

Ym mhob crefft y mae ffalster
There's a trick in every trade

Hwy darogan gwaith na'i wneud
It takes longer to talk about work than to do it

Ni bu'r bostiwr erioed yn weithiwr
The boaster was never a worker

Odid difro diwyd
The diligent are rarely away from their community

Cyfoethog i werthu, tlawd i brynu
Go to the rich to sell and the poor to buy

Dau dalu drwg: talu 'mlaen a pheidio â thalu
Two bad forms of payment: paying beforehand and not
paying at all

Diwedd dydd y mae profi gŵr
A workman is judged at the end of the day

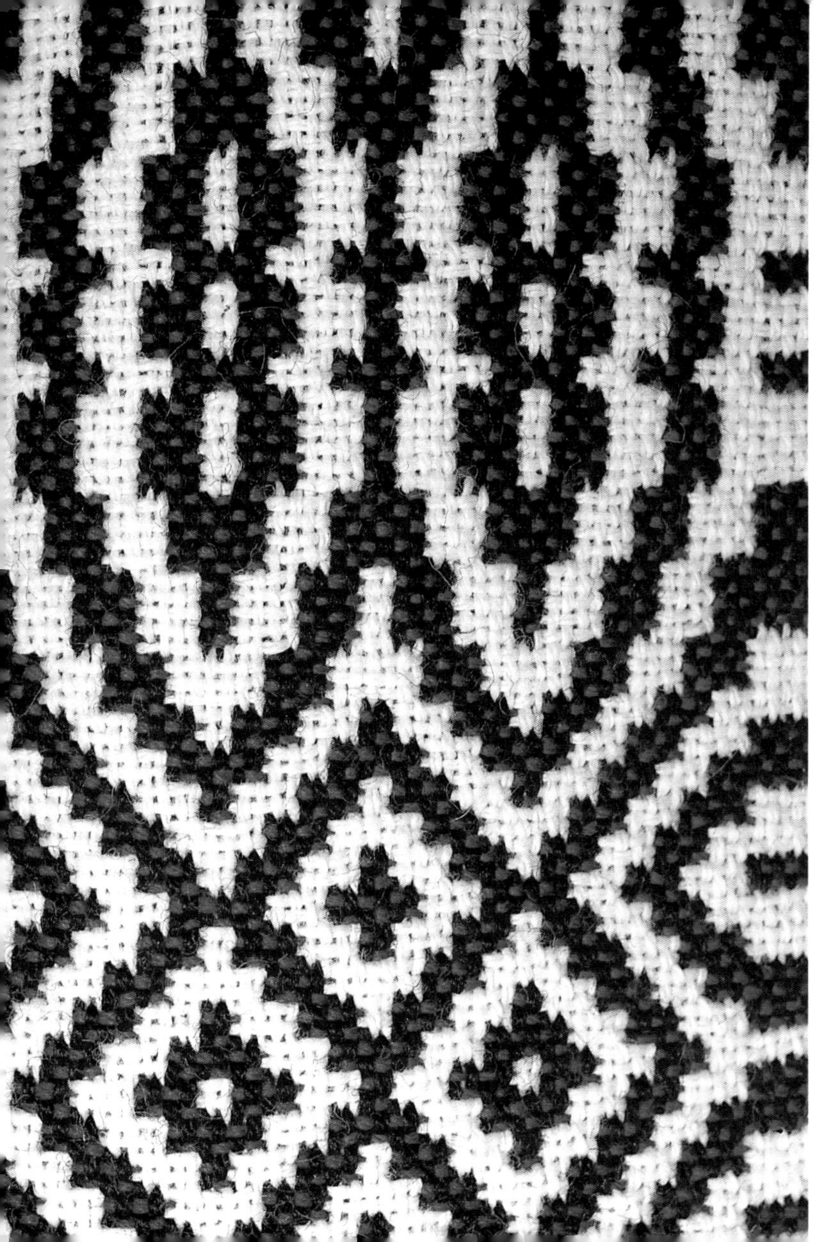

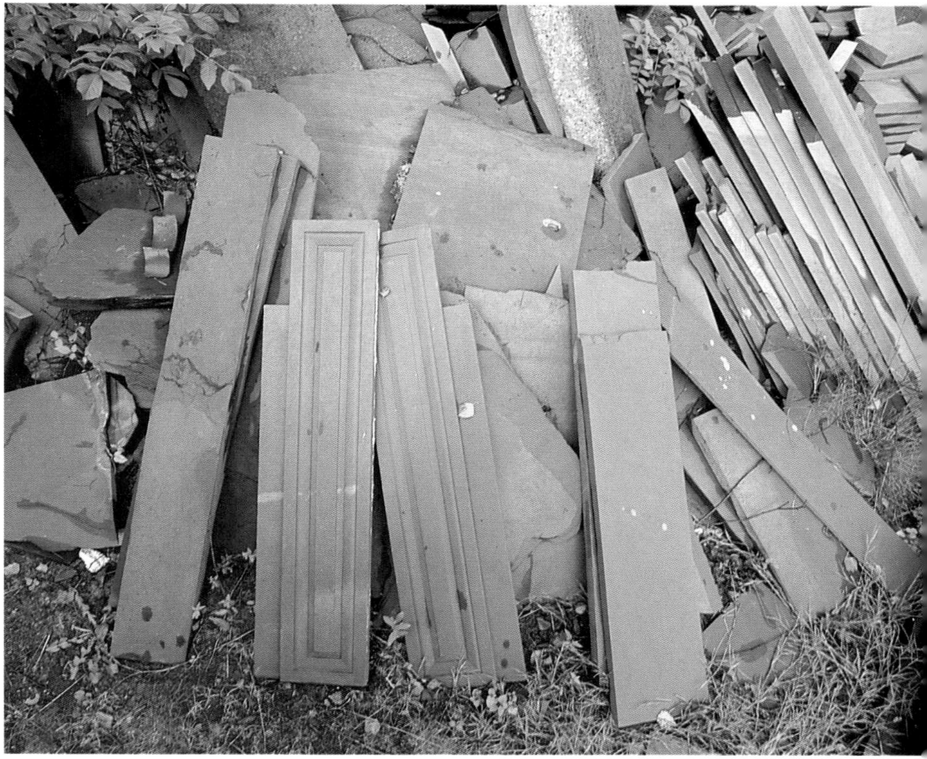

Y CYBYDD / THE MISER

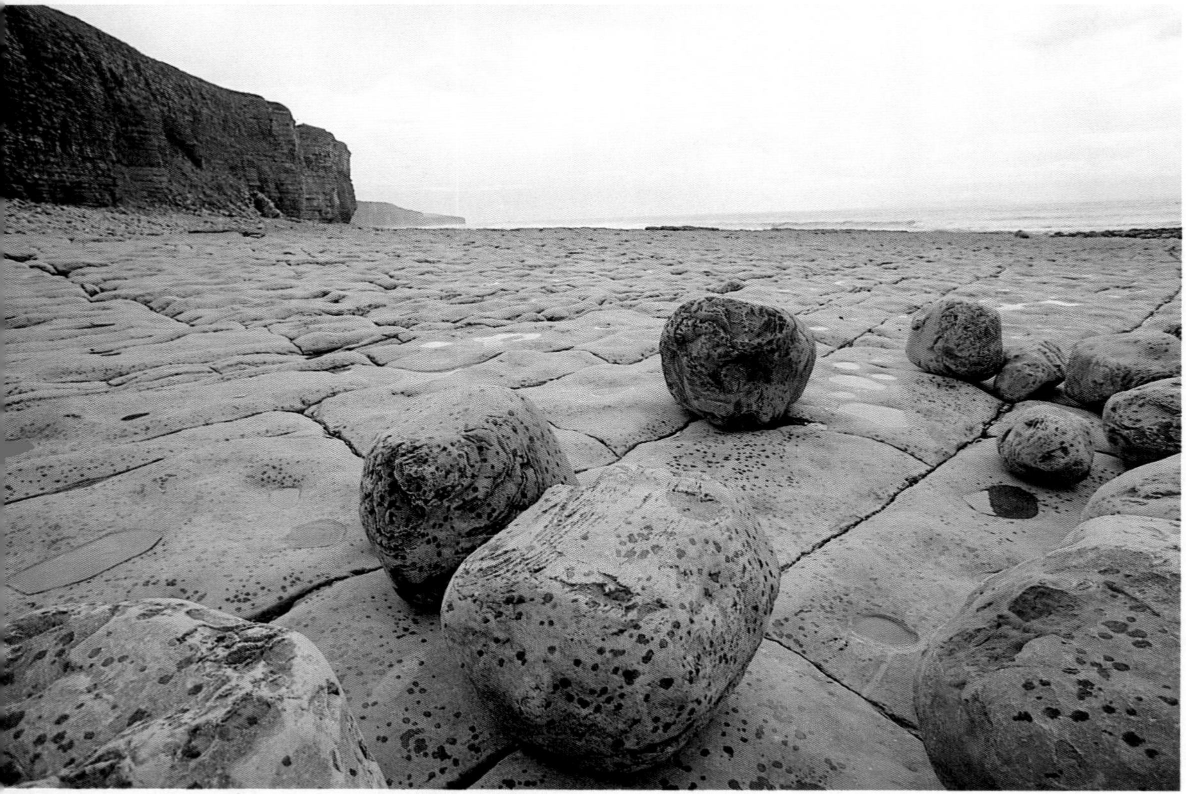

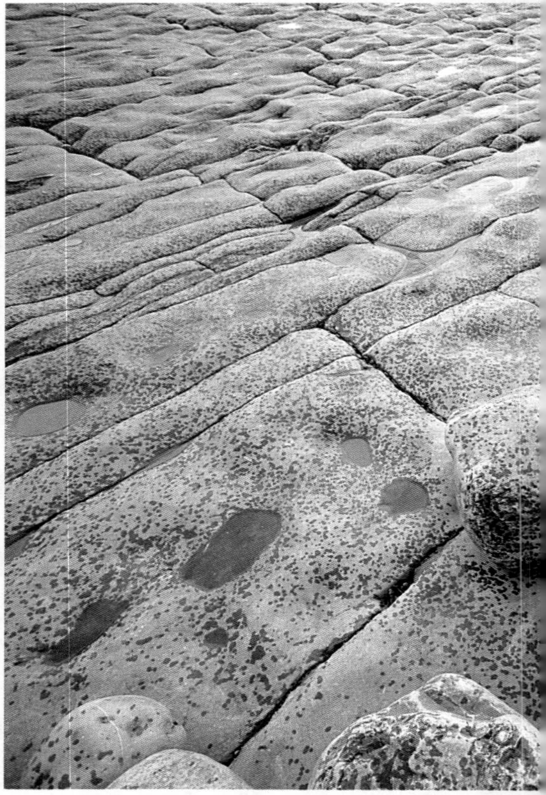

Throughout the Celtic world, great emphasis was placed on generosity, so the miser was treated with the utmost contempt. There are few allusions to misers in Welsh literature or records, and it is almost as if the concept itself were so abhorrent that people were fascinated by it - as the number of proverbs suggests.

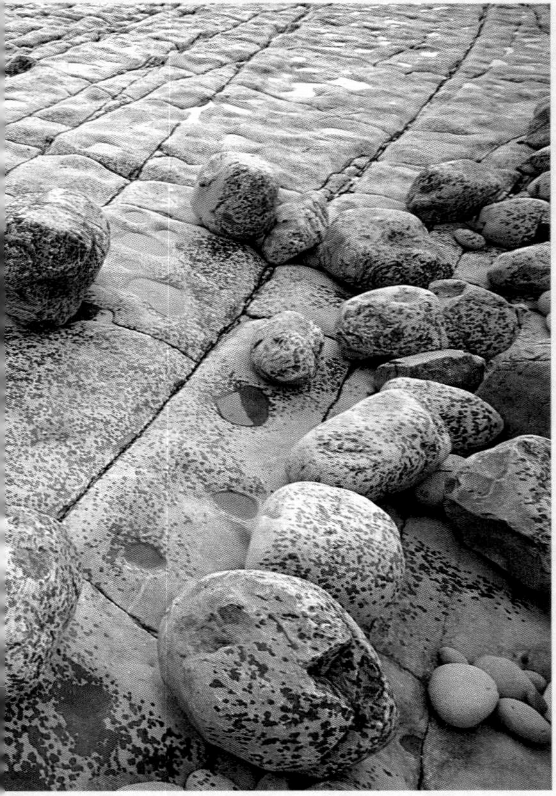

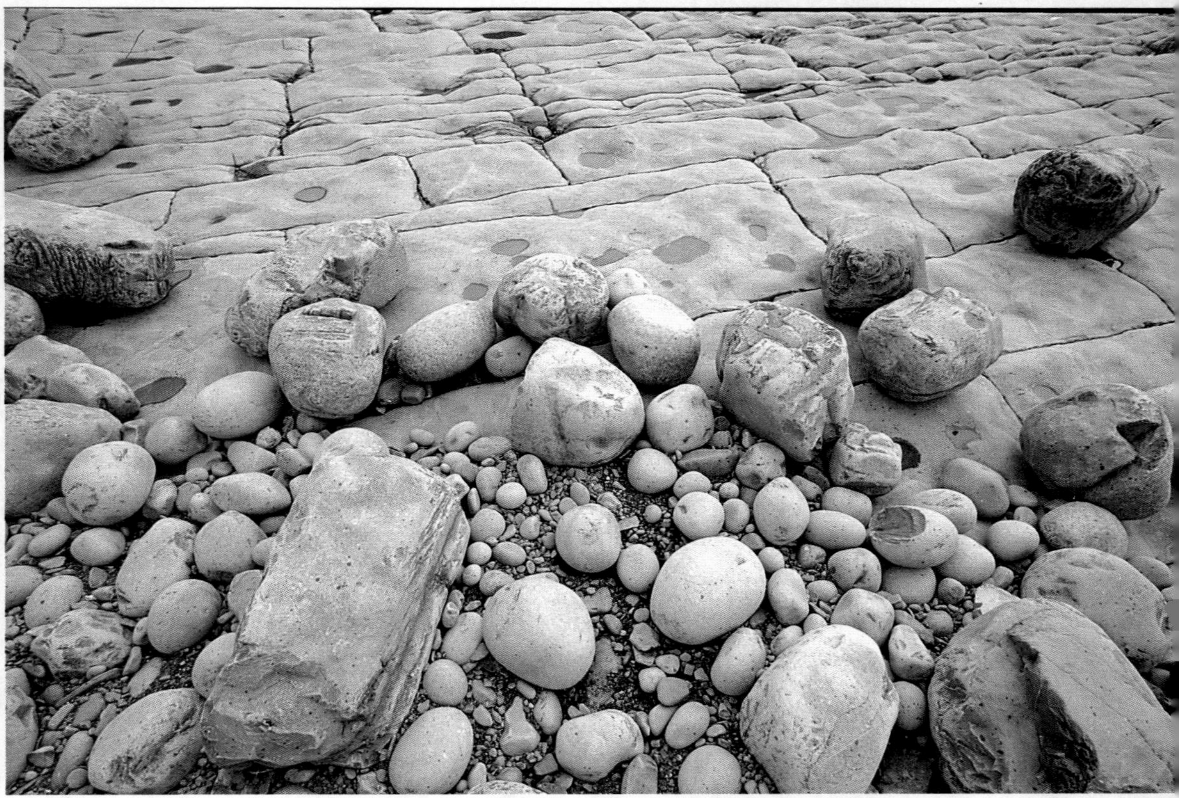

Tri chaled byd - maen callestr, corn hydd hefryn a chalon mab y crinwas

Three hard things of the world - flint, gelded buck's horn and the miser's heart

Tri oer byd: trwyn milgi, maen clais ac aelwyd mab y crinwas
Three cold things of the world: a greyhound's nose, marble and a miser's hearth

Gwell corog na chybydd
Better a generous man than a miser

Cybydd a wna geiniog yn swllt,
Hael a'i gwna'n ganswllt
A miser will turn a penny into a shilling,
The generous will turn it into a hundred

Gwell cynnwys cotyn na lleidr
Better welcome a miser than a thief

Nid cybydd yw pob caled
Every hard man is not a miser

Ni ddygymydd medd a chybydd
Mead and the miser do not agree

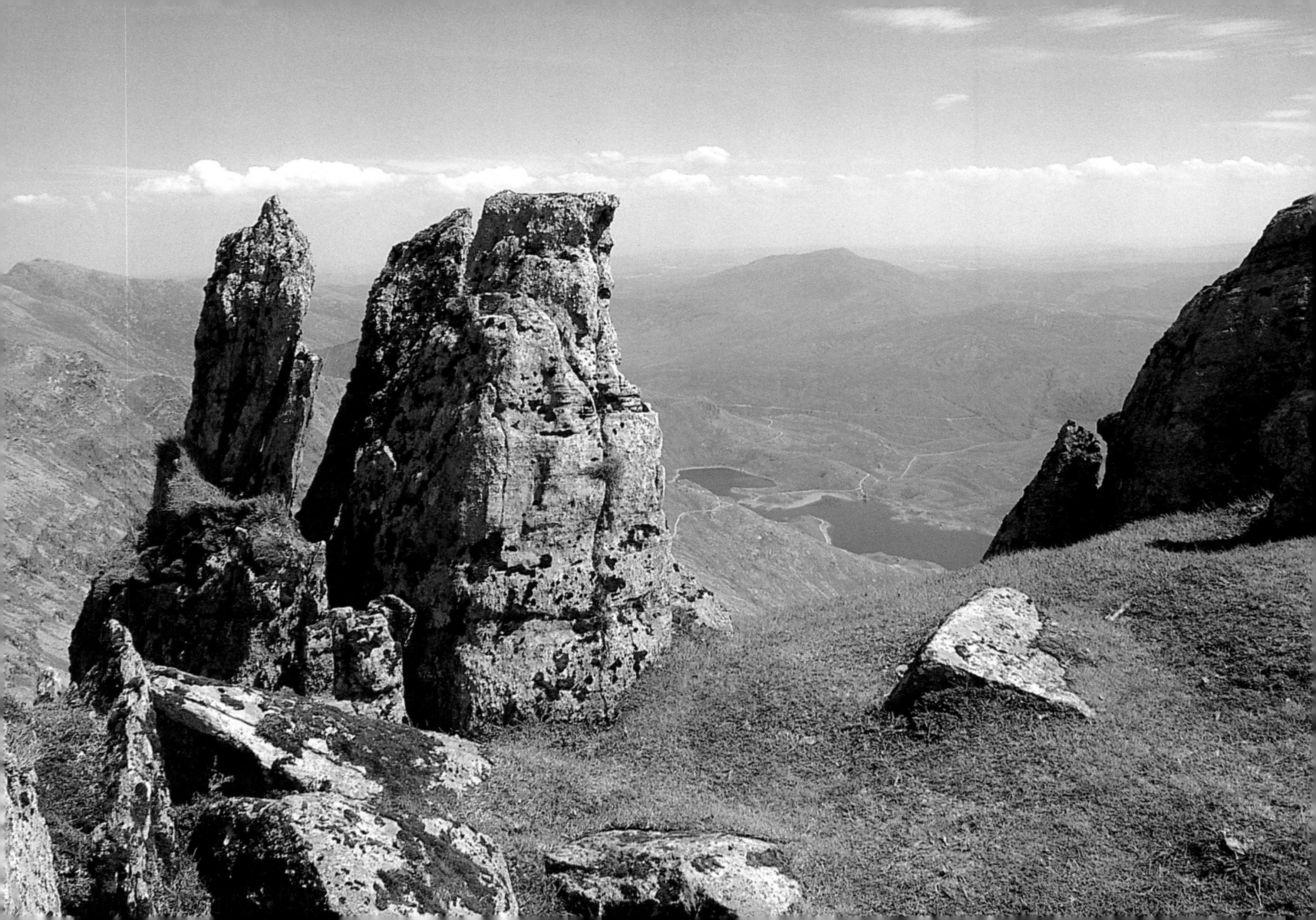

YR YNFYD / THE FOOL

If we thought that mental illness or 'different-ness' were modern phenomena we would be wrong. Traditionally, simplicity and madness were factors of every community, as the number of proverbs testifies.

Neither is community care a new concept; during most of man's existence the immediate community has been the framework within which the mentally ill have been accepted and cared for. Although labelled 'idiot' and 'fool', they were known by everyone, often given simple jobs, and their role in society was assured.

Ateb y ffŵl yn ôl ei ffolineb
Answer the fool according to his folly

Tri chwerthin ffŵl - am ben y da, am ben y drwg ac am ben nas gŵyr pa beth
Three things at which a fool laughs - what is good, what is bad and what he cannot understand

Doeth dwl tra tawo
A fool is wise when quiet

Cas gan ynfyd a'i cynghoro
The fool hates his advisers

Llwydd ac ynfyd ni ddygymydd
Success and a fool cannot be reconciled

Mae barn gan ffŵl, ond barn ffŵl yw hi
A fool has an opinion but it is the opinion of a fool

Ni chêl ynfyd ei feddwl
A fool does not hide his thoughts

Ni ddawr croesan ei gabl
The buffoon fears not to blaspheme

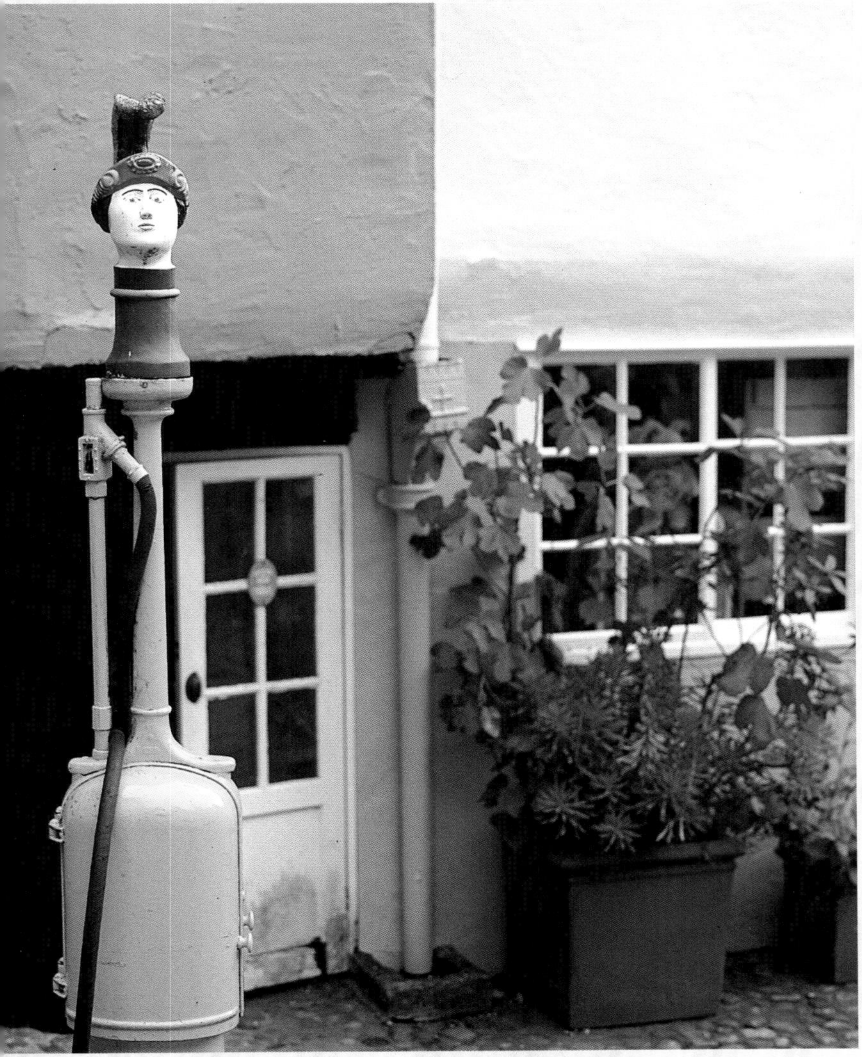

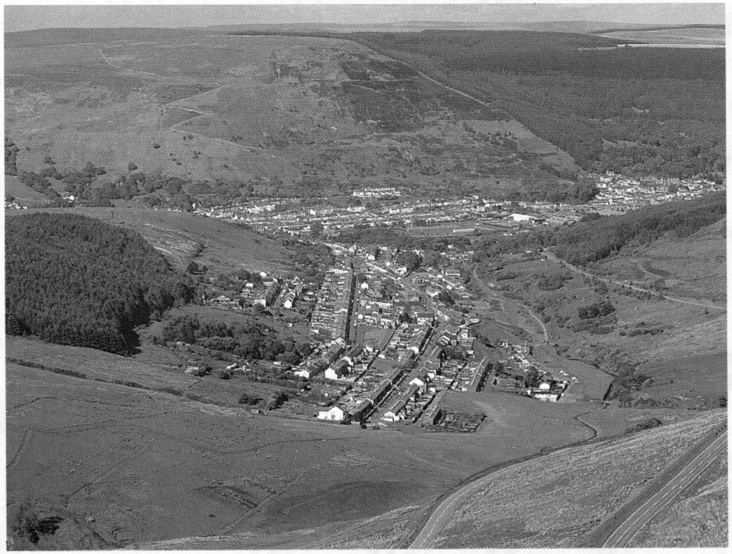

Nid â cosb ar ynfyd
A fool is not punished

Llwyddiant yr ynfyd a'i ladd yn y diwedd
The fool's success will kill him in the end

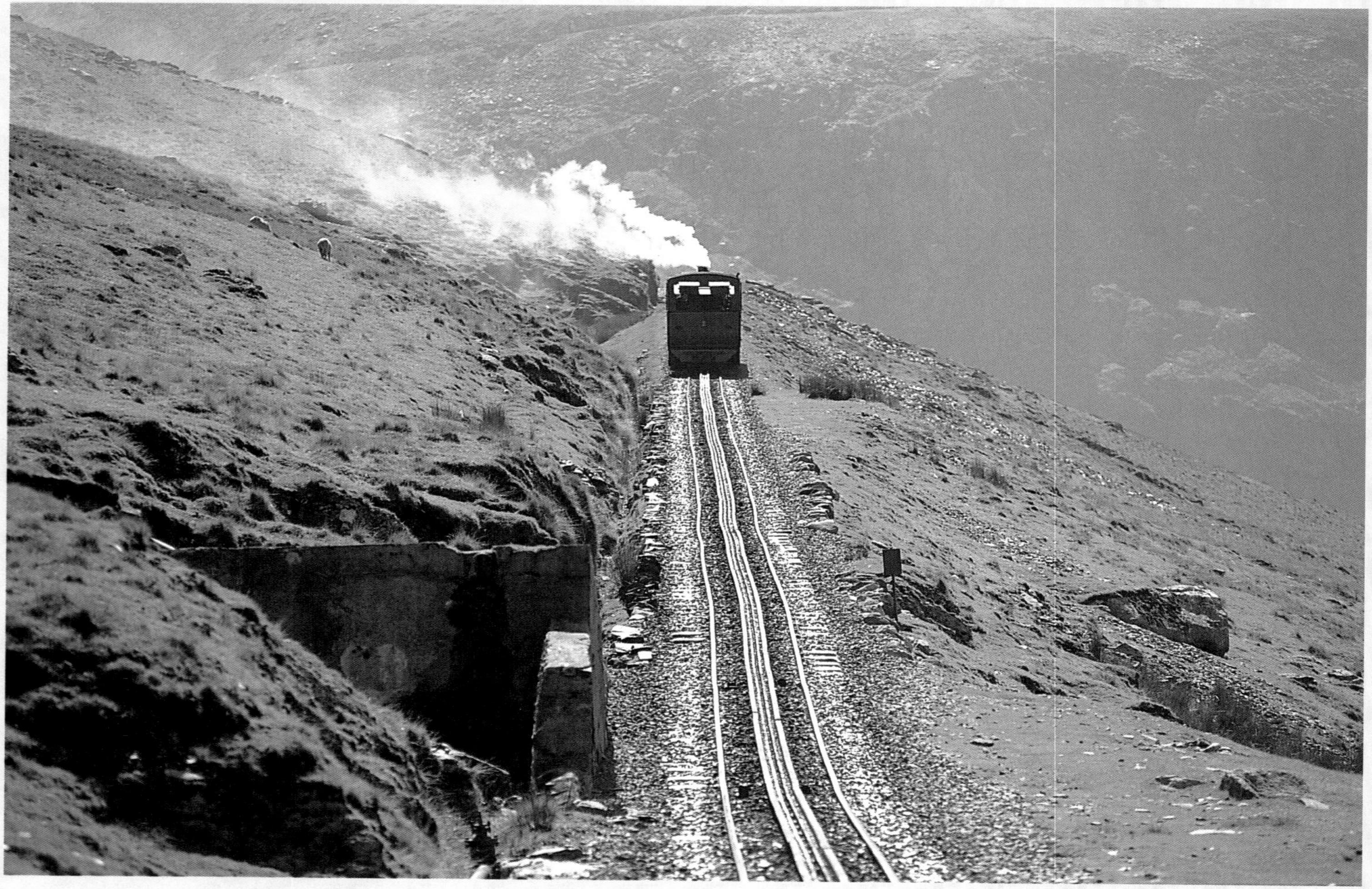

From the departure of the Romans in the fifth century, right up to the construction of the toll roads in the eighteenth century, no major public road building took place in the whole of Britain. Travel was rarely undertaken except when absolutely necessary - in fact, the word travel comes from the French 'travail' which means to work and even the word journey comes from the French 'journeé', meaning the amount of work or the distance covered in a day. The idea of travelling simply for pleasure, as we know it, is quite a modern one.

DAVID LLOYD GEORGE

Ni wŷr dyn nid êl o'i dŷ
A man who does not leave home will learn nothing

Hanner y daith, cychwyn
Half the journey is starting

Ci a gerddo a gaiff
The dog that walks will get

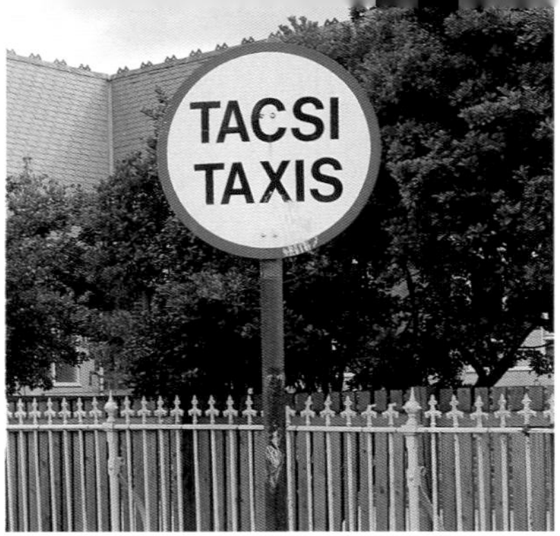
TACSI
TAXIS

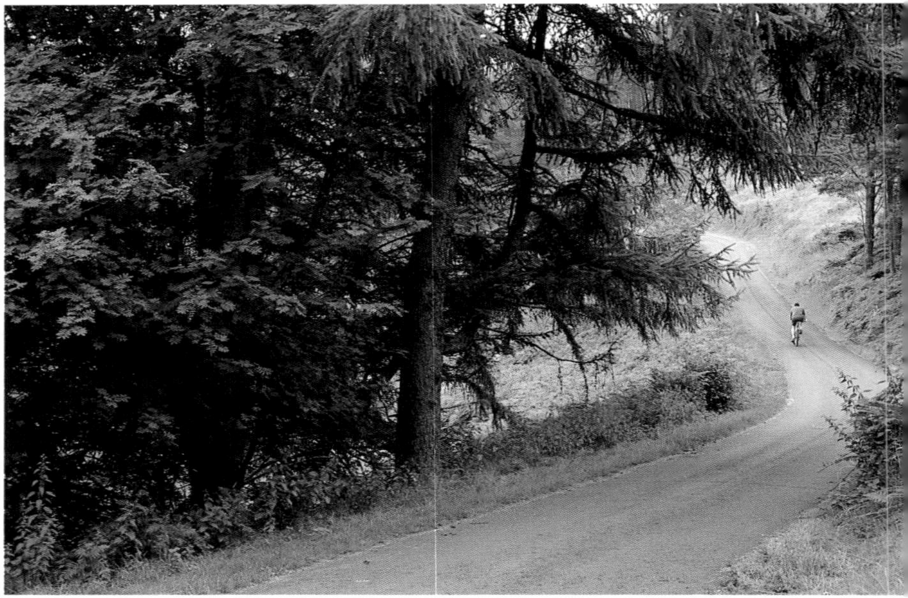

Hir yw'r ffordd nis cerddwyd ond unwaith
The road is long that has been travelled only once

Gan bwyll y mae mynd ymhell
Going steadily one travels far

Edwyn dyn ei gydymaith ar daith hir
A man gets to know his companion on a long journey

Ffŵl a grwydra, doeth a deithia
A fool wanders, the wise travel

Teg edrych tuag adre
It is fair to look homewards

Y sawl a fu a ŵyr y fan
He who has been will know the place

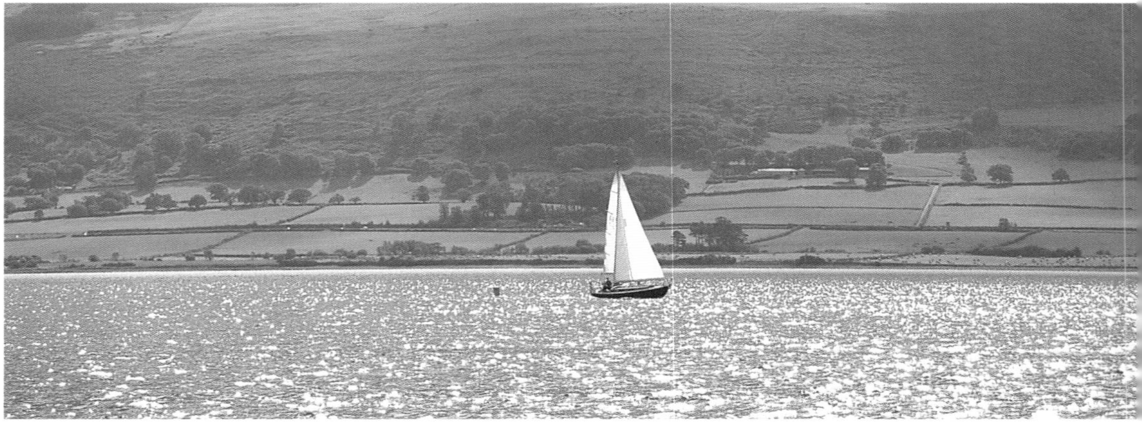

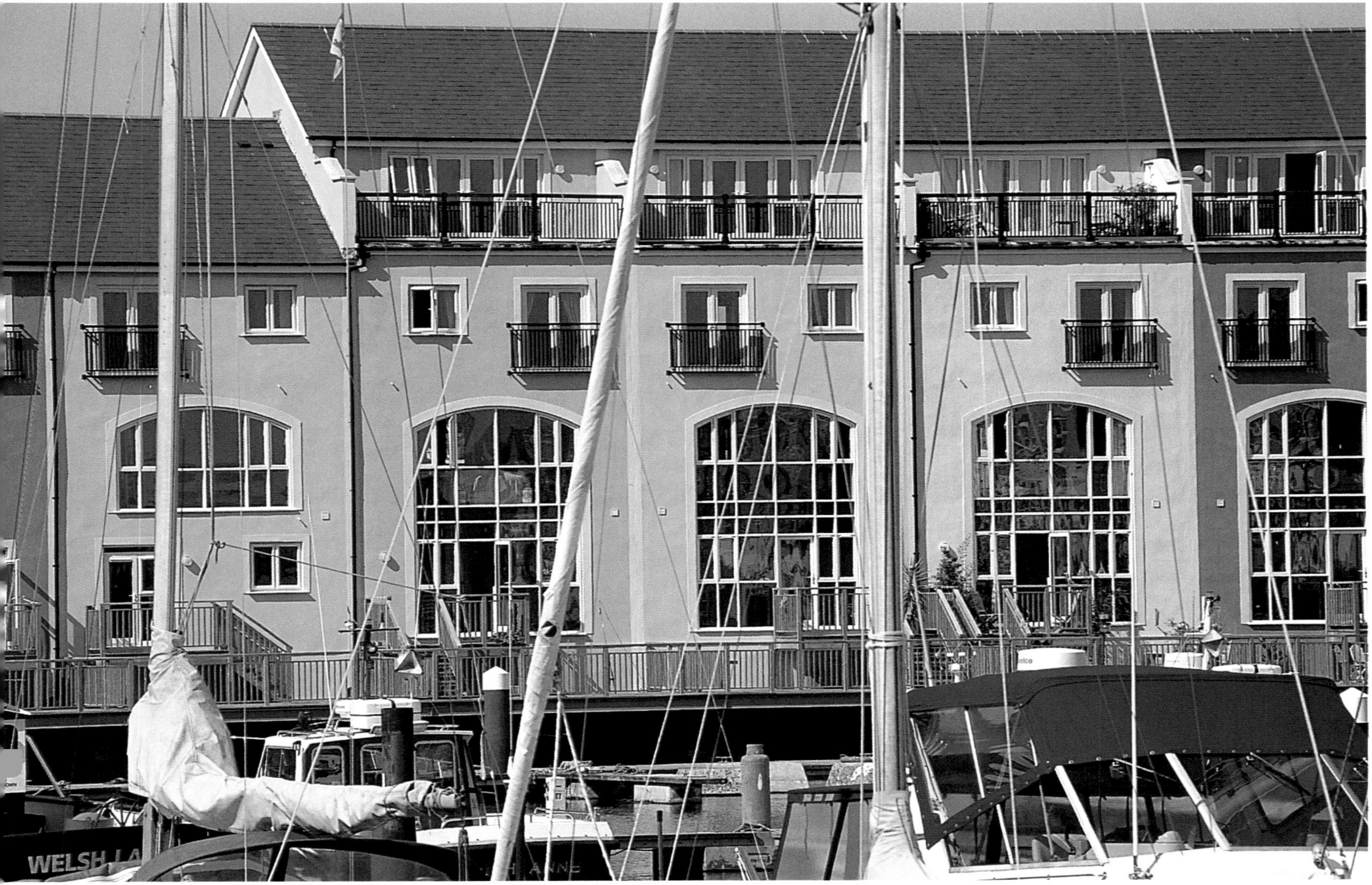
WELSH

pike Roads, Highways, or Bridges; Horses or Carriages emp
ying Manure (save Lime) for improving Lands, or Ploughs, or in
andry; Horses employed in Husbandry, going to or returning f
or from Pasture, or Watering place, or going to be or returnin
d, and Horses not going or returning on those occations
niles on the Turnpike Road on which the exemption is claimed; P
returning from, their proper parochial Church or Chapel, Perso
rning from, their usual place of religious worship tolerated by
ays, or on any day on which Devine Service is ordered to be
itants of any Parish or Township going to, or returning from at
al of any Person who shall die or be buried in the Parish, Townsh
any turnpike Road shall lie, any Rector, Vicar, or Curate, on his pa
n his Parish; Horses, Carts, or Waggons, conveying Vagrants sent
risoner sent by legal warrant; Horses or Carriages conveyin
s of any Officer or Soldier on march or duty; Horses or Carria
rms or Baggage of any such Soldiers or Officers, or returnin
ick, Wounded, or disabled Officers, or Soldiers, or any Ordnance,
s; Horses and Carriages used by Corps of Yeomanry or Volunte
ages carrying or conveying any person to and from Coun
Horse carrying any Agricultural produce which shall have gr
occupation of, or cultivated, used, or enjoyed by the Ow
uce, and which shall not have been sold; Sheep going t

CYSYLLTIADAU / COMMUNICATIONS

It is now difficult to imagine a world without mass communications, but even up until the First World War the majority of people had very little idea what was happening in the rest of the country, let alone the rest of the world. News was often brought by the drovers, who travelled England and Wales taking animals to markets, where Welsh livestock was greatly prized. In the nineteenth century news was also disseminated by ballad-singers, who sang about current events and sold their ballad sheets.

Na ro goel i newyddion oni bônt yn hen
Do not believe news unless it is old

Cred air o bob deg a glywi, a thi a gei rywfaint bach o wir
Believe one word in ten you hear, and you will get a little truth

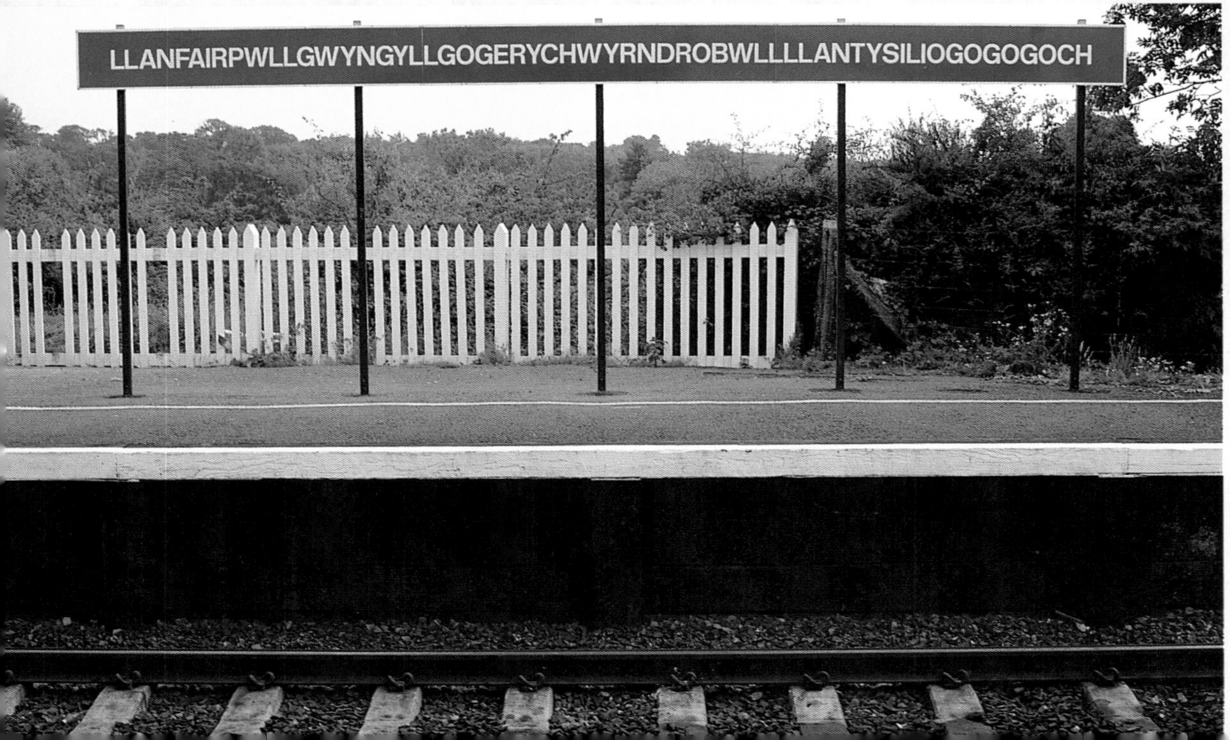
LLANFAIRPWLLGWYNGYLLGOGERYCHWYRNDROBWLLLLANTYSILIOGOGOGOCH

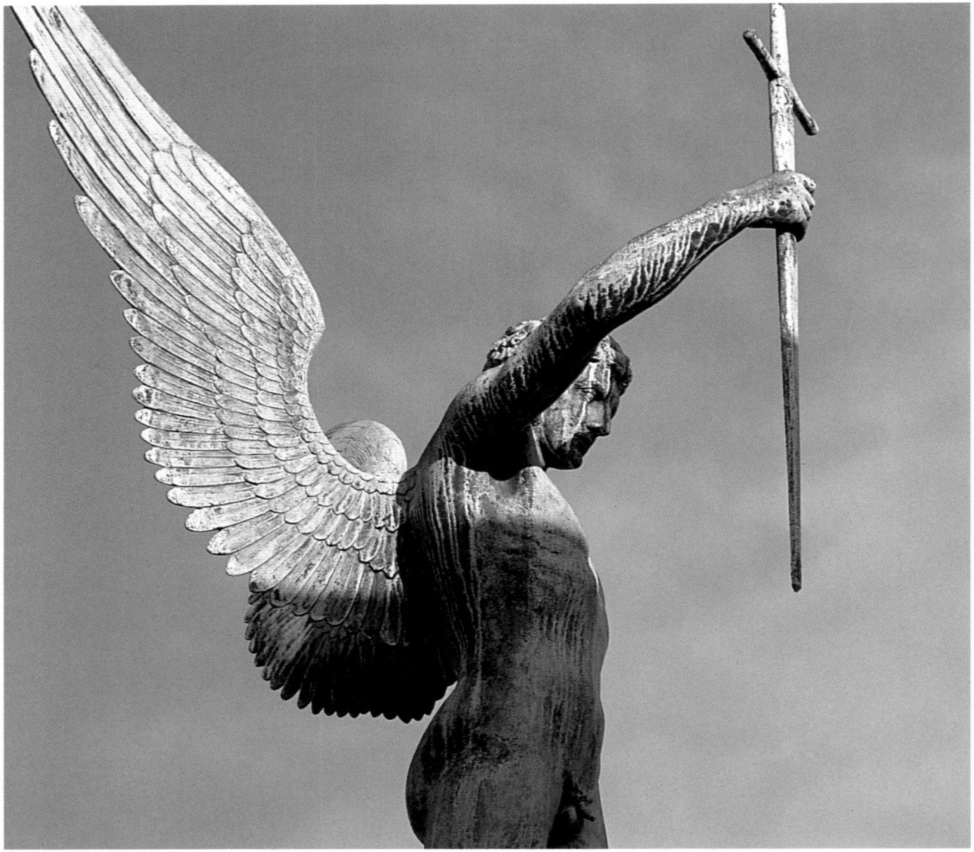

Nac adrodd a glywaist rhag ei fod yn gelwyddog
Do not repeat what you heard in case it is untruthful

Nid yw chwedl yn colli wrth ei hadrodd
A tale does not lose through the telling

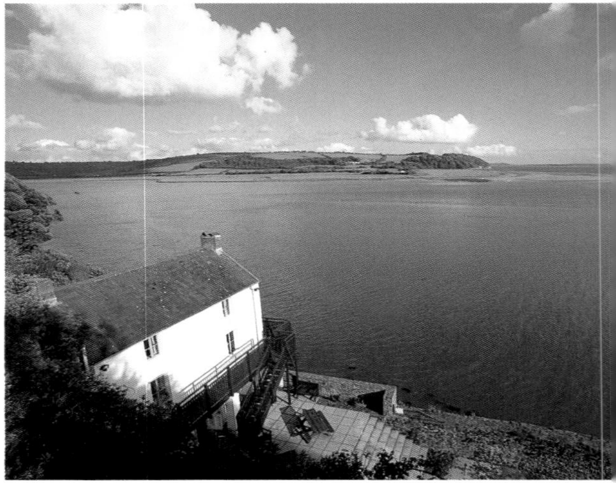

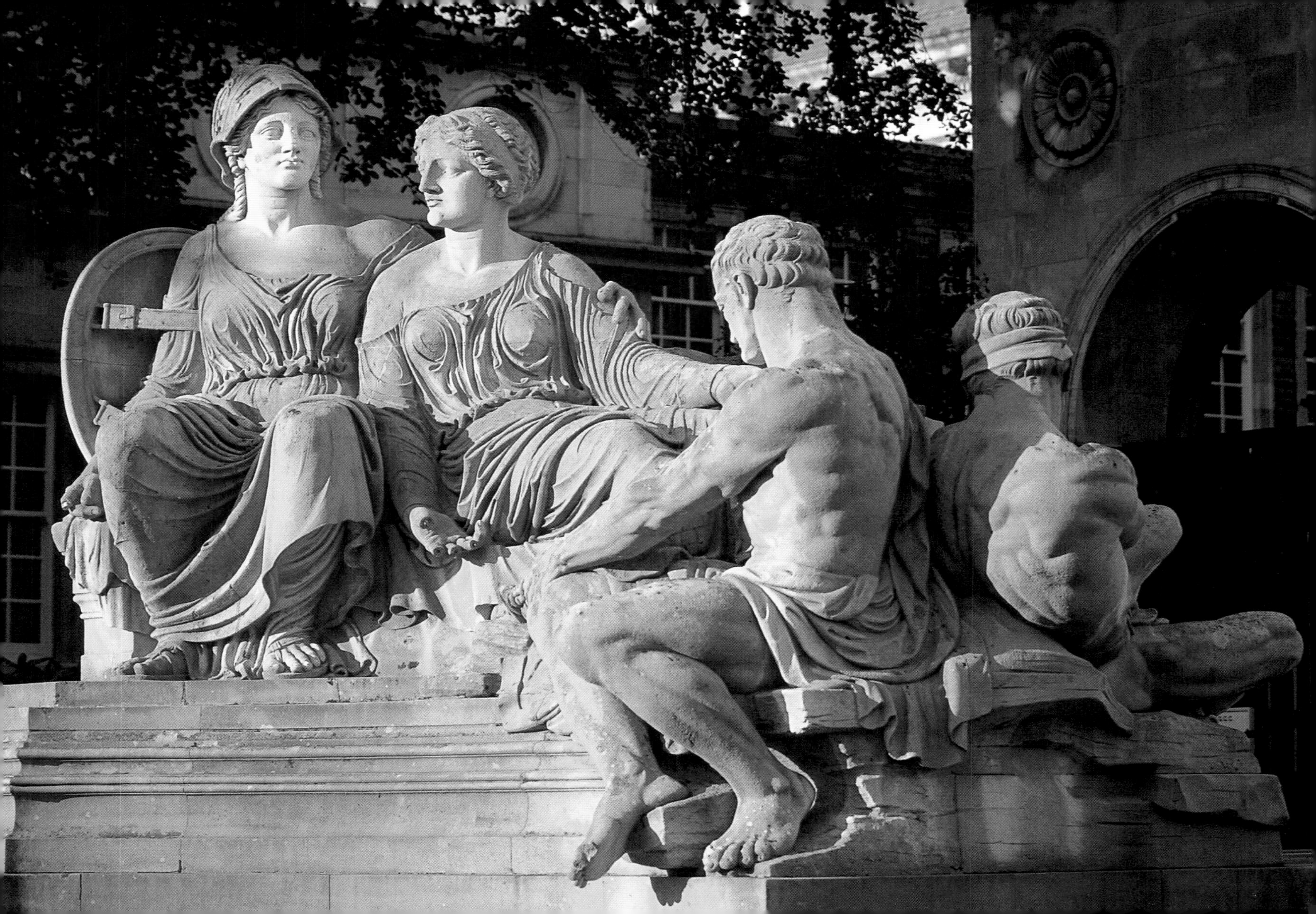

PENDEFIGAETH A'R CYFOETHOG / ARISTOCRACY AND THE WEALTHY

Most Welsh proverbs show a disdain and mistrust of the gentry that can only have been bred from an unhappy relationship with them!

Cyfoeth a chwanega lawer o gyfeillion
Wealth makes many friends

Allwedd arian a dyr bob clo
A silver key will open all locks

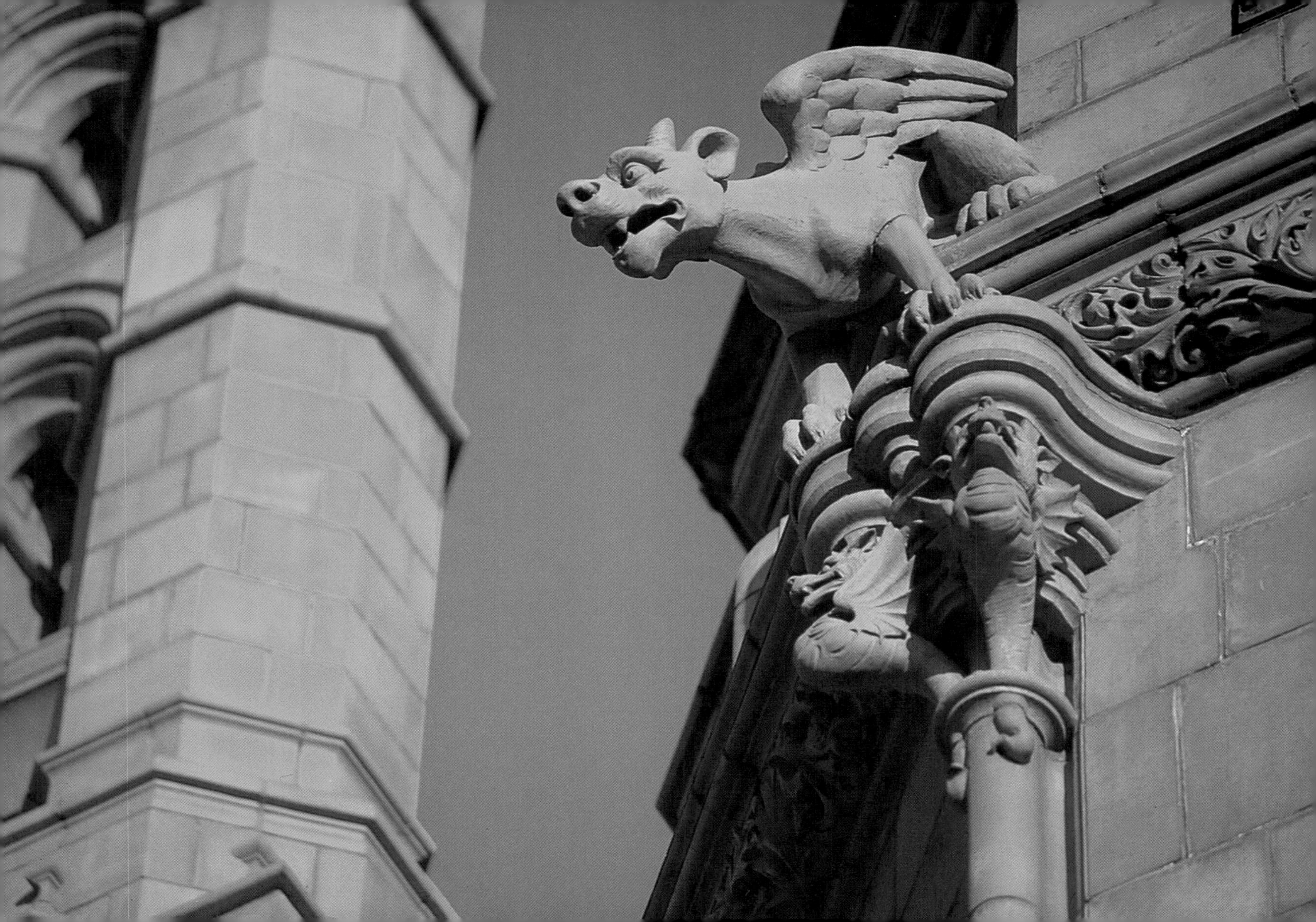

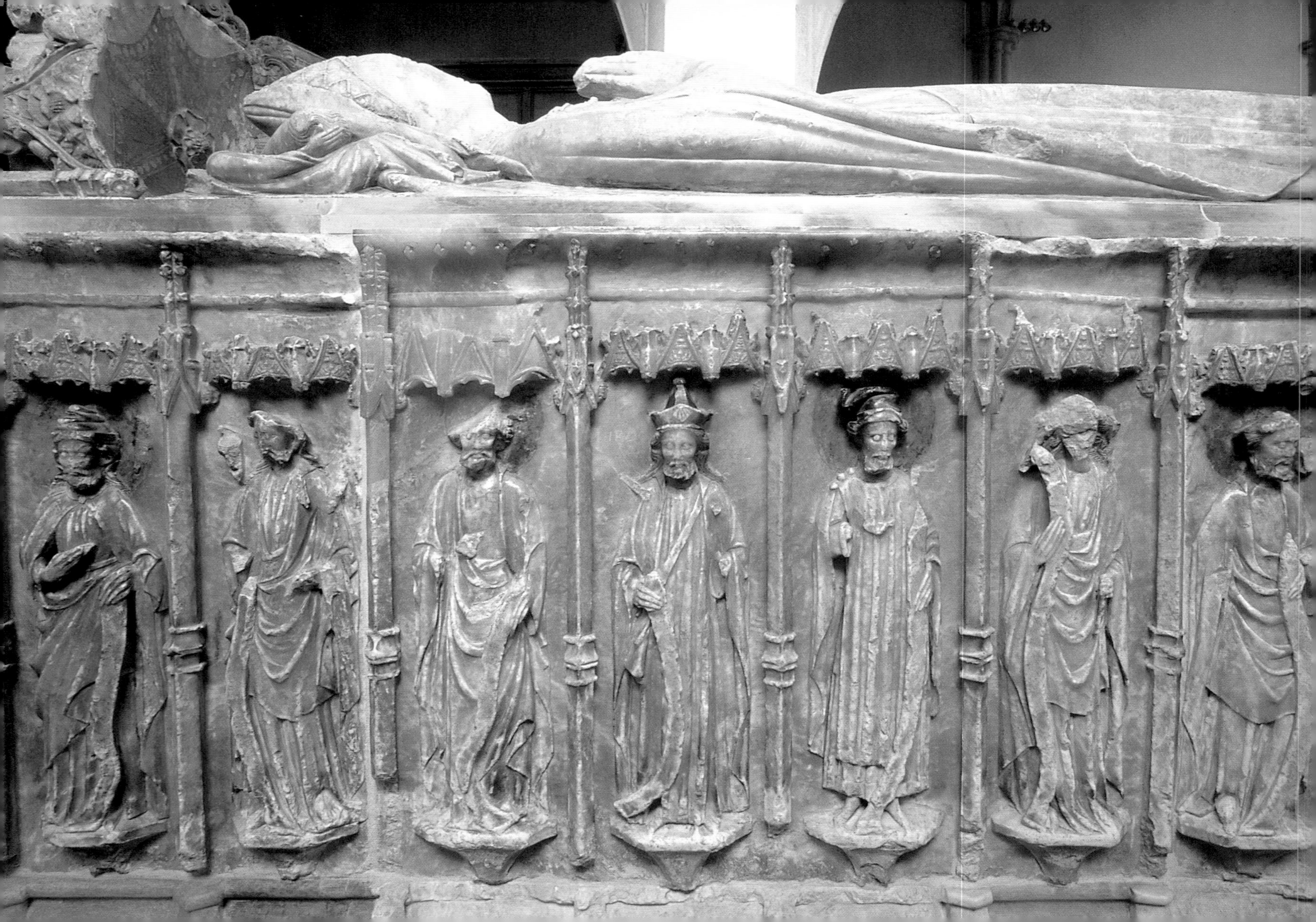

Mae'r goludog yn ymfrasâu ar ddagrau y tlodion
The wealthy get fat on the tears of the poor

Traha a threisio'r gweinion a ddifa'r etifeddion
The oppression of the weak is the destruction of heirs

Cydfwyta â mab arglwydd, ac na chydchwarae
Eat with a lord's son but do not play together with him

O gyfoeth y daw gofid
From wealth comes worry

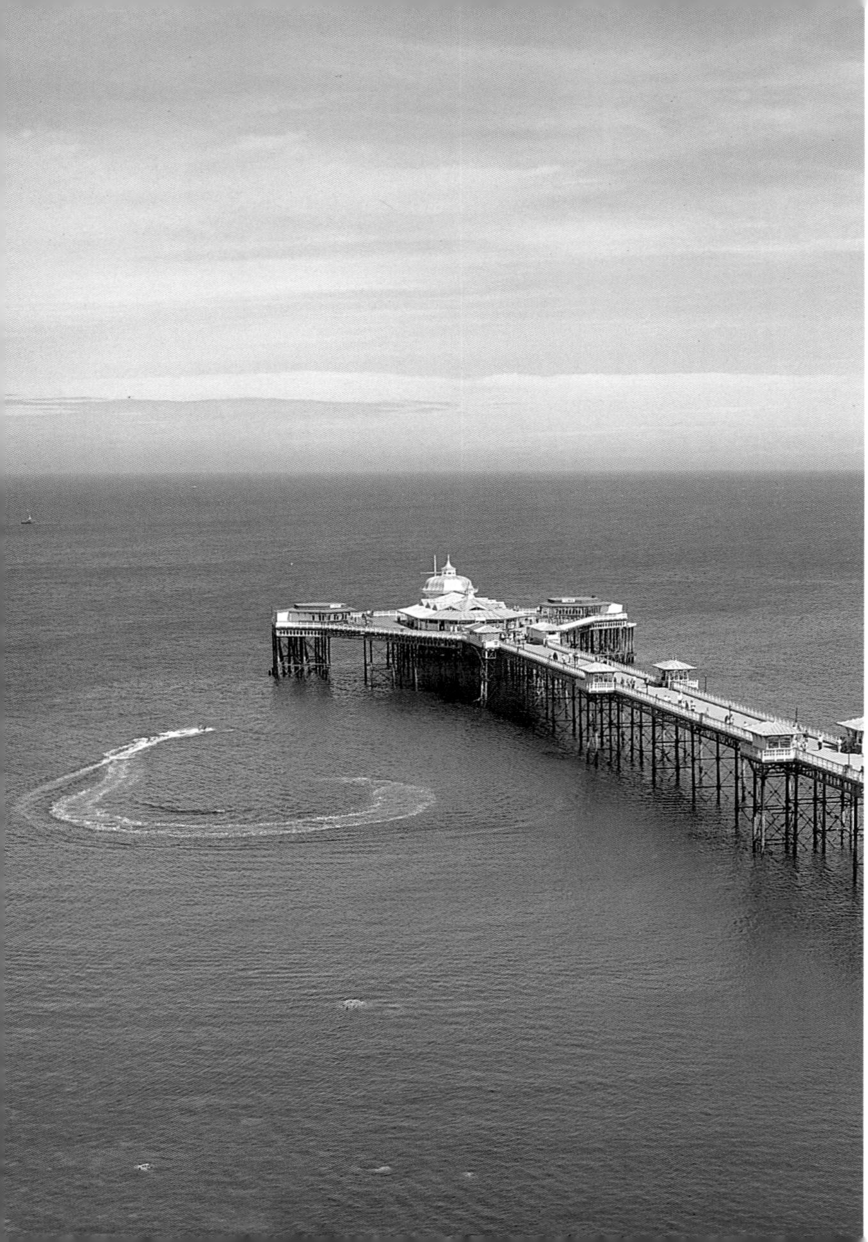

The Mostyn family still owns land in north Wales, including Llandudno, which is perhaps the best example of an Edwardian resort in Britain.

'*Mae mistar ar Mistar Mostyn*
Master Mostyn has a master

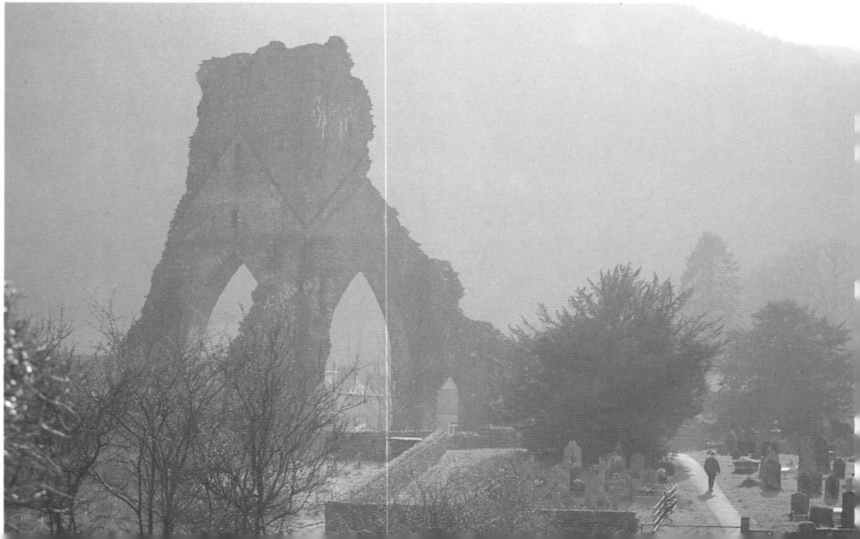

Y BRENIN ARTHUR / KING ARTHUR

Arthur is probably one of the greatest mythical figures in the world. He is first mentioned in the Welsh epic poem, the Gododdin, which was composed in the seventh century and is the earliest British poem in existence.

The Annals of Wales were written in 960 but were made up of much earlier material; they say that in 518, at the British victory of Baddon, Arthur carried the cross of Christ on his shoulder, and in 539 Arthur and Medrawd fell at Camlann. In the Historia Brittonum, written at the beginning of the ninth century, the Welsh monk, Nennius, attributes many victories over the Saxons to Arthur; and in the body of Welsh literature known as The Mabinogion, Arthur takes part in many adventures, including hunting a magical boar and making a journey into the Celtic Otherworld, Annwfn.

However, it was Geoffrey of Monmouth, writing in the twelfth century, who set the seal of respectability on Arthur in the history of the British race. The Historia Regum Britanniae (the History of the Kings of Britain) had the effect of ensuring Arthur's worldwide fame up to the present day. It is, therefore, natural that he and his companions, like Merlin, are mentioned in proverbs and connected to many places in Britain.

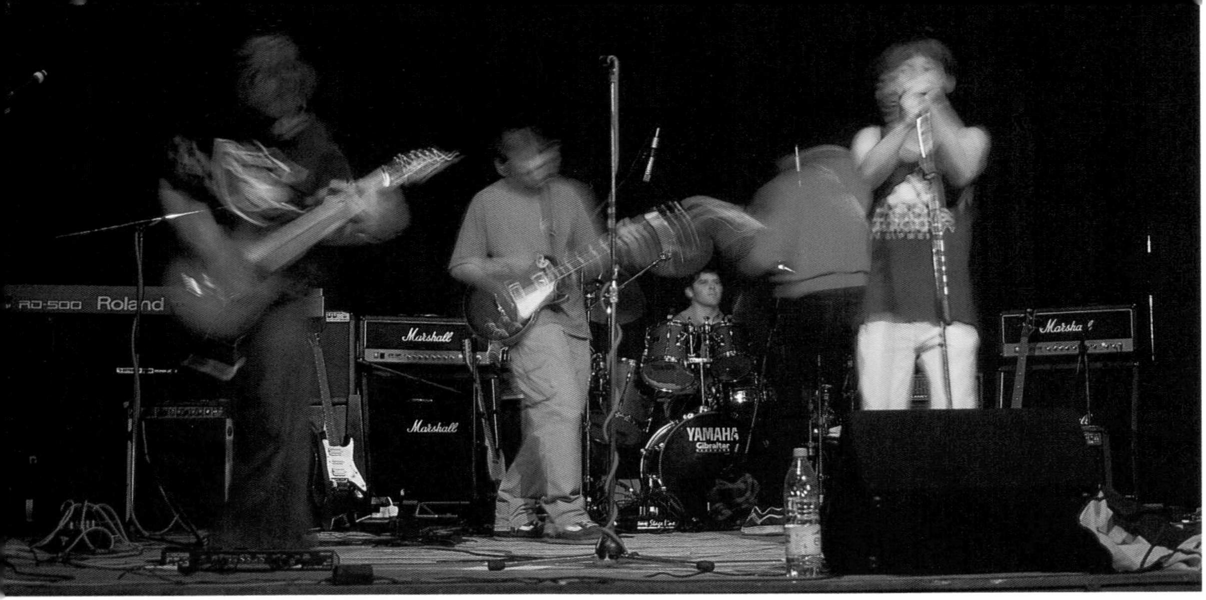
RD-500 Roland
Marshall
Marshall
YAMAHA
Gibraltar
Marshall

Ni bu Arthur ond tra fu
Even Arthur only was when he was

I neuadd Arthur, namyn mab brenin gwlad teithiog, neu gerddor a ddyco ei gerdd, ni ater i mewn
Into the court of King Arthur there is no entry, save for the travelling son of a king and a musician who brings his music

Ni thorres Arthur nawdd gwraig
Arthur never broke a lady's protection

Siarad cymaint â Myrddin ar bawl
To talk as much as Merlin on a stake

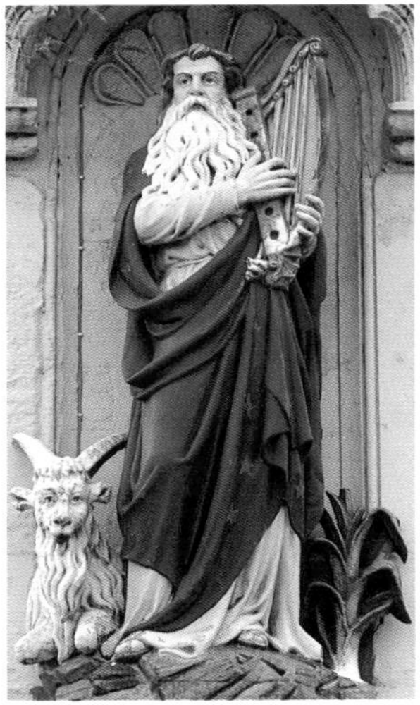

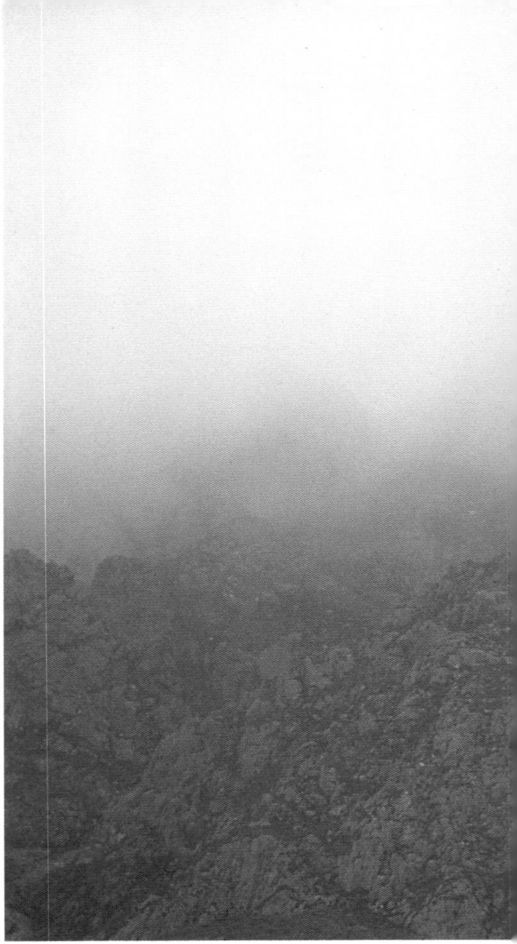

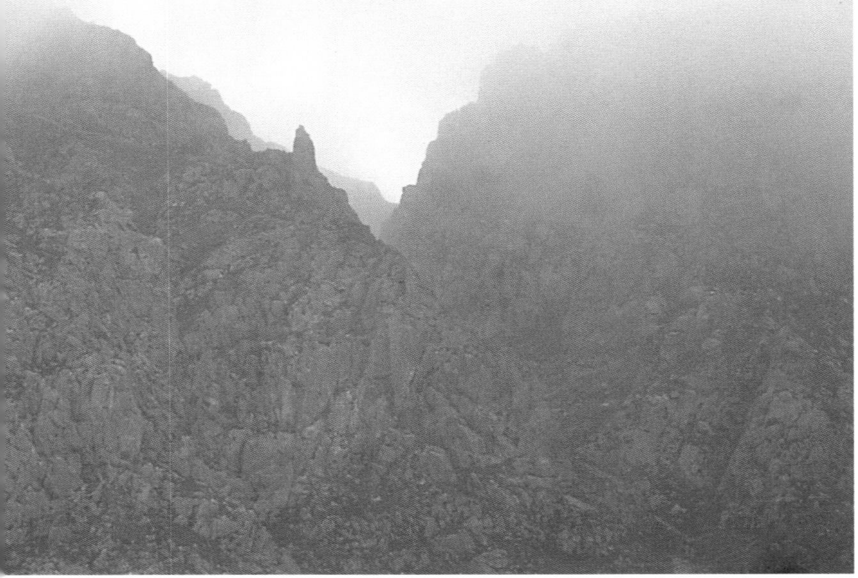
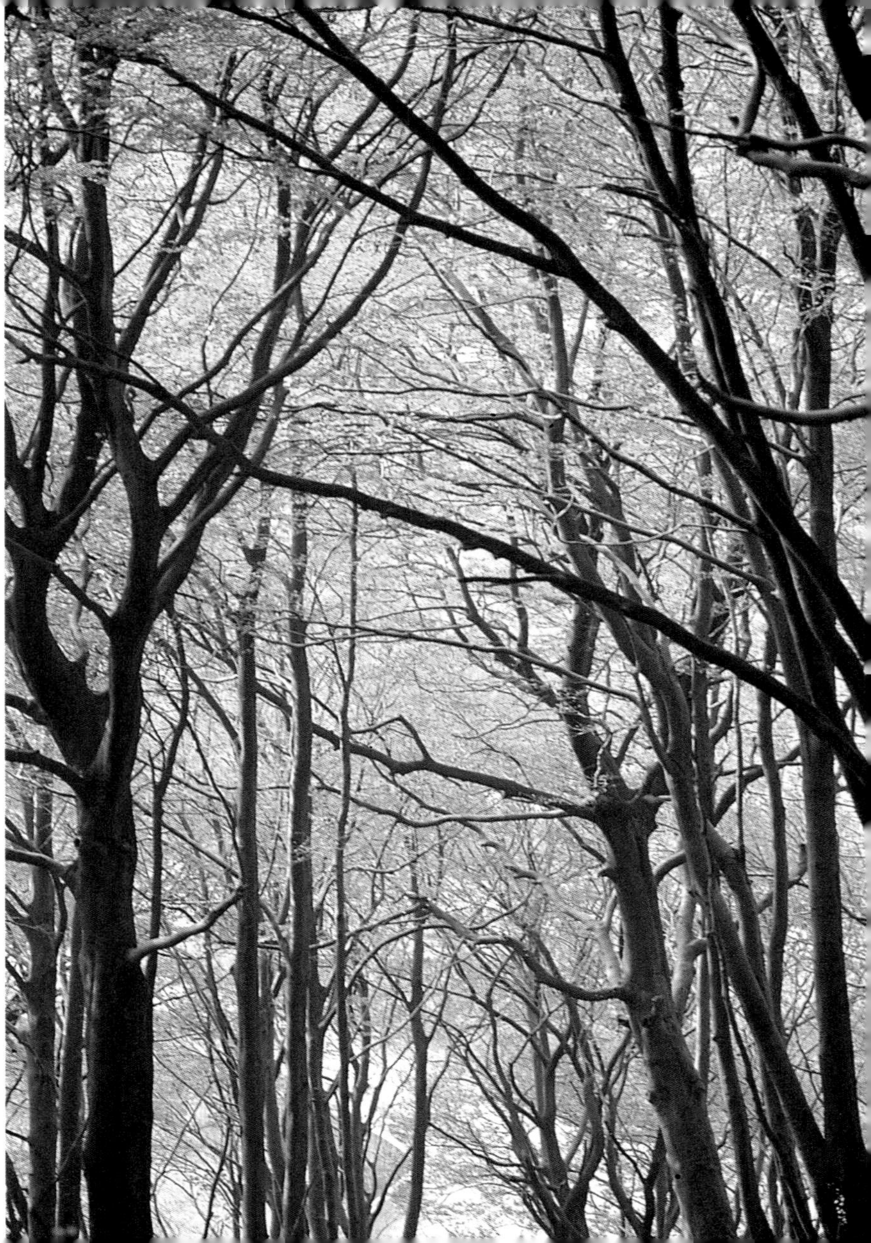

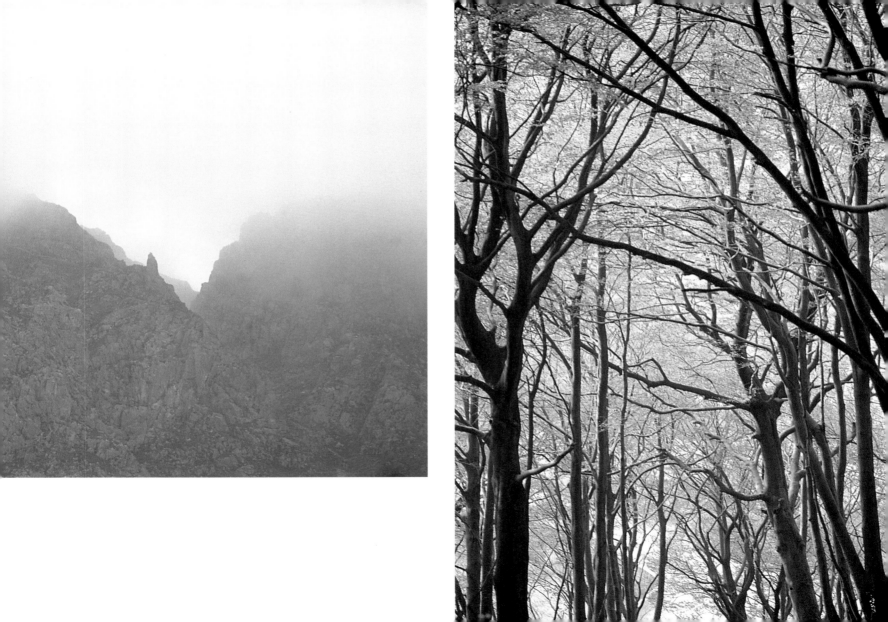

TRIOEDD / TRIADS

Classical authors say that it took twenty years to train a Druid and that their seat of learning was in Britain. Their whole body of knowledge was committed to memory, not because they were unable to write - there are examples of Druidic writing, using both the Latin and Greek alphabets - but because they were afraid that the uninitiated would take possession of it. They, therefore, had to find ways of making it easy to memorise their many laws, genealogies and beliefs about earth and the heavens. It is thought that the triads was one way of doing this.

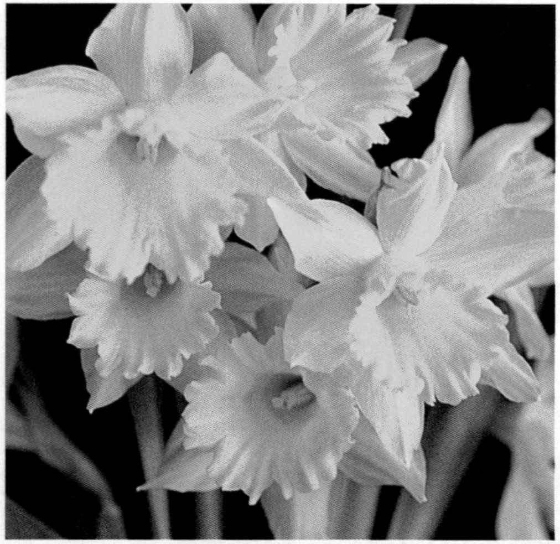

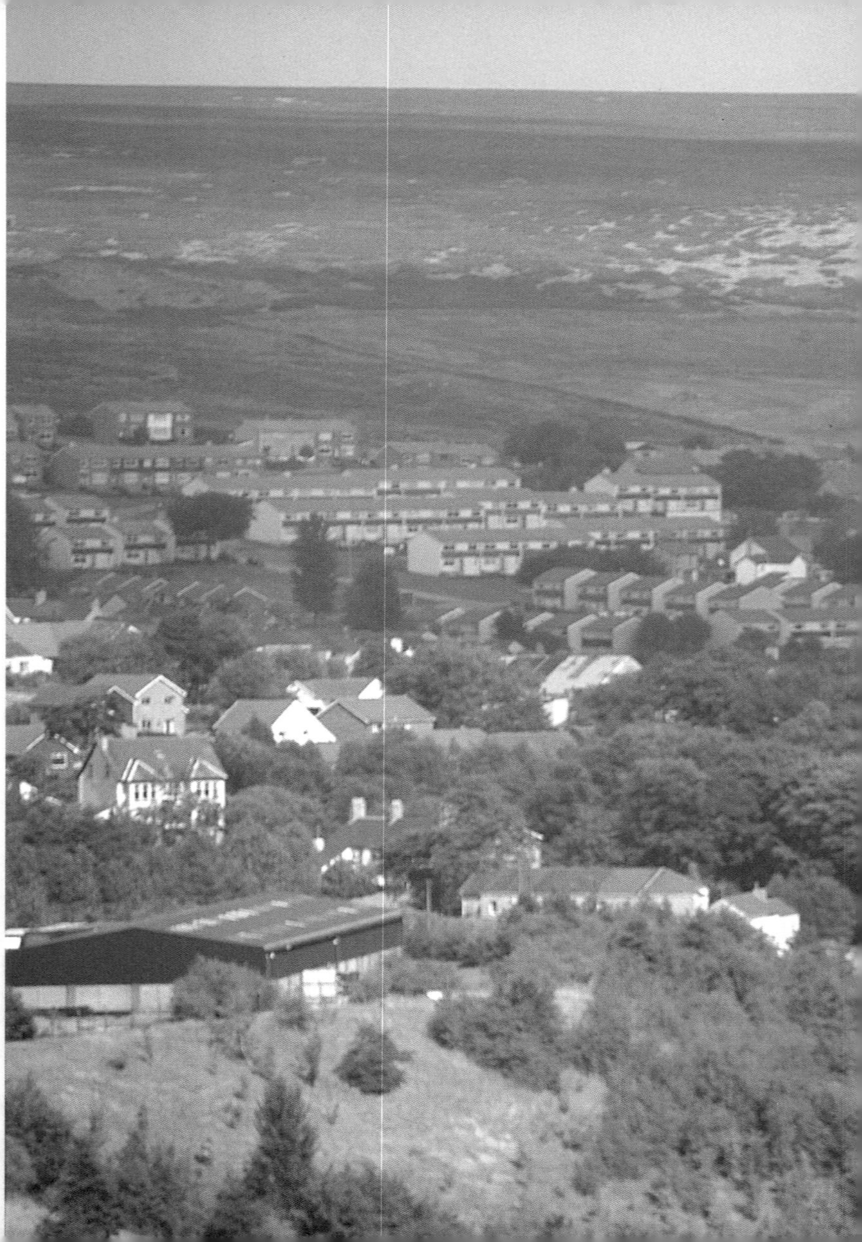

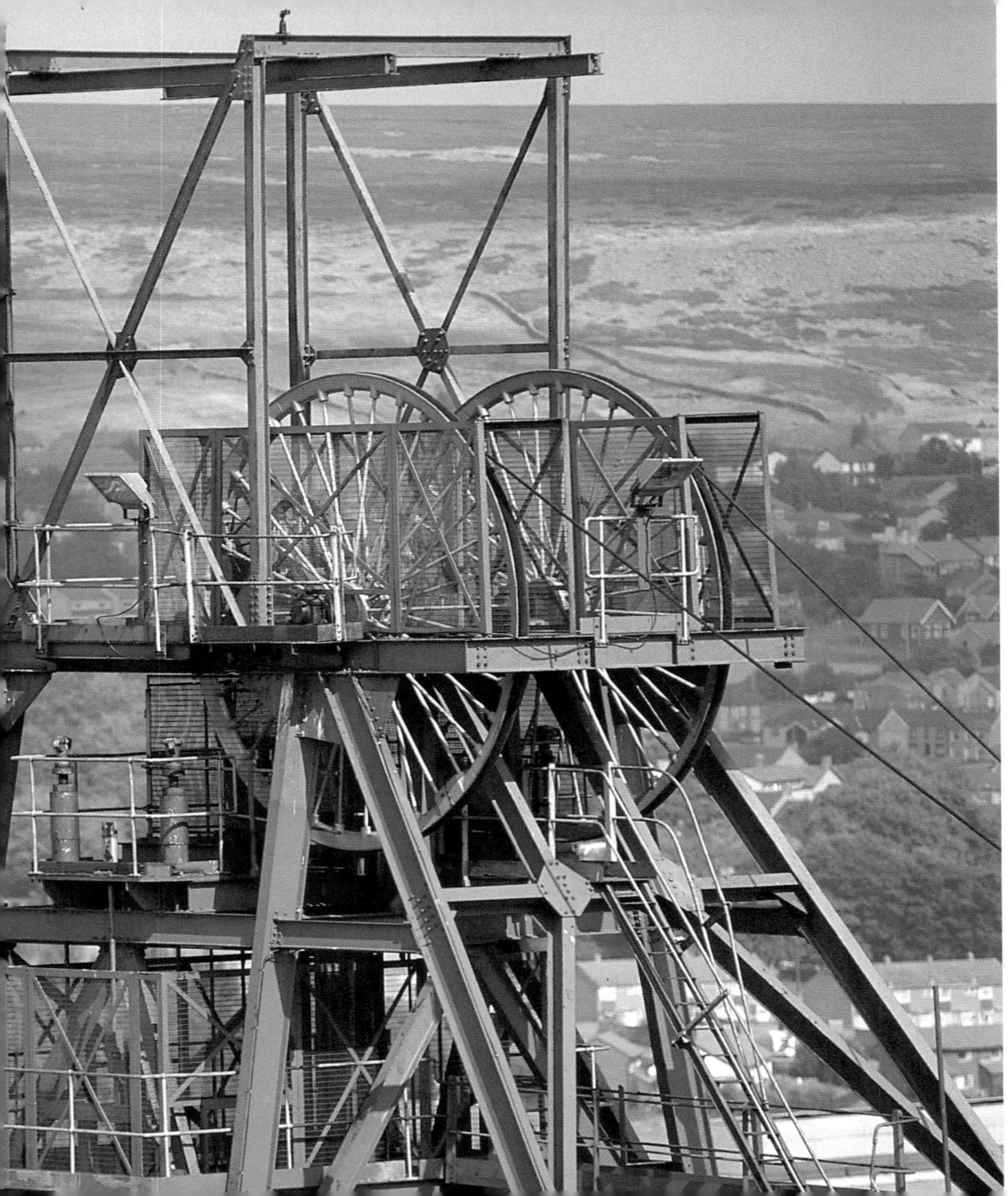

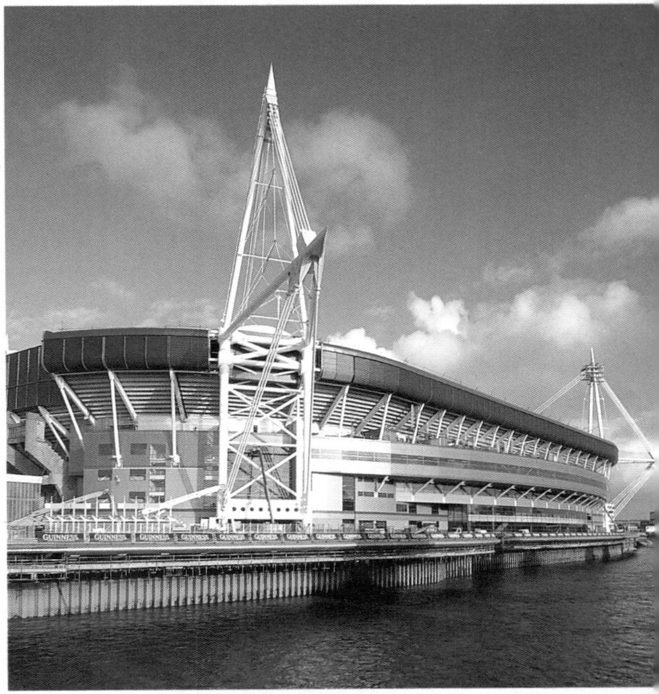
GUINNESS

Tri pheth y dylem eu caru - aroglau meillionen, blas llaeth a chân adar y coed
Three things we ought to love - the fragrance of clover, the taste of milk and the song of woodland birds

Tri chynhaliaeth awen - llwyddiant, cydnabyddiaeth a chanmoliaeth
Three things that maintain the muse - success, acknowledgement and praise

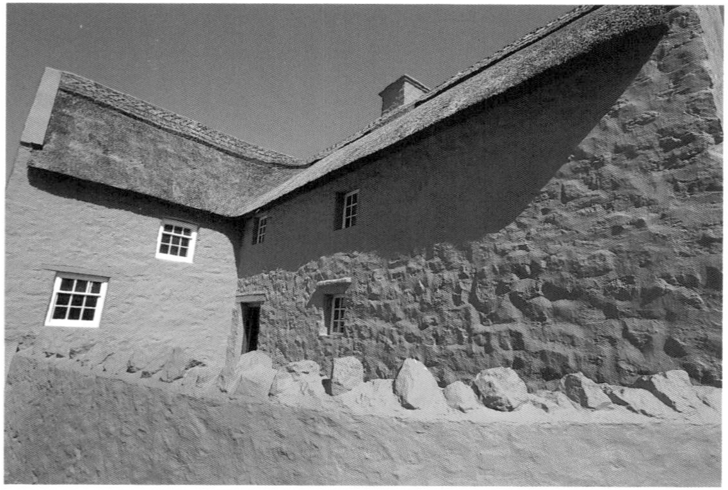

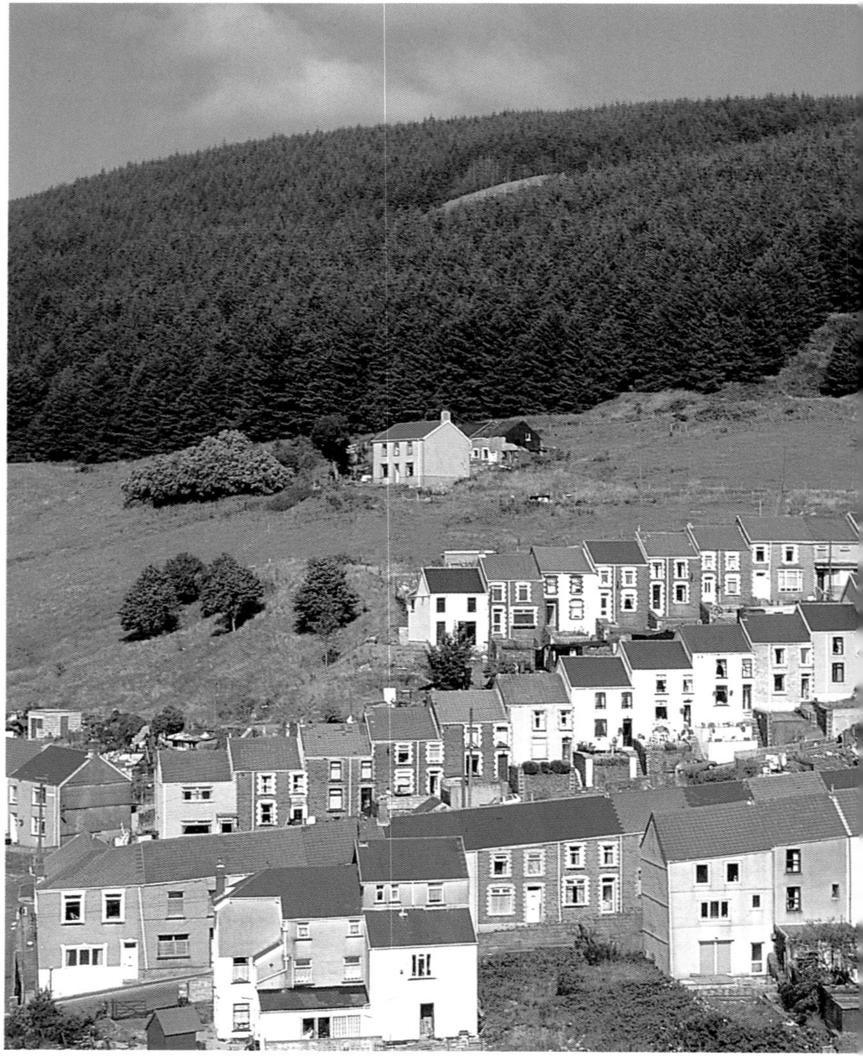

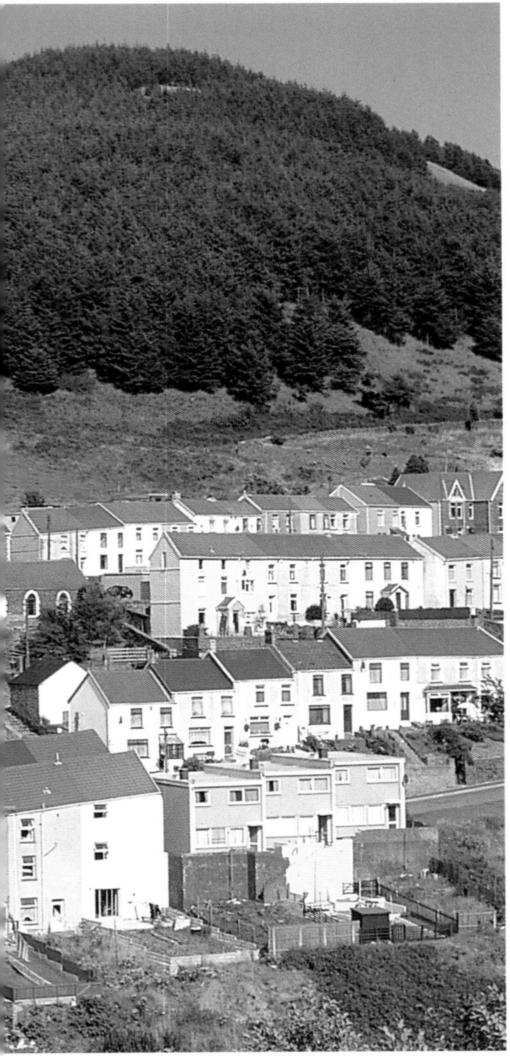

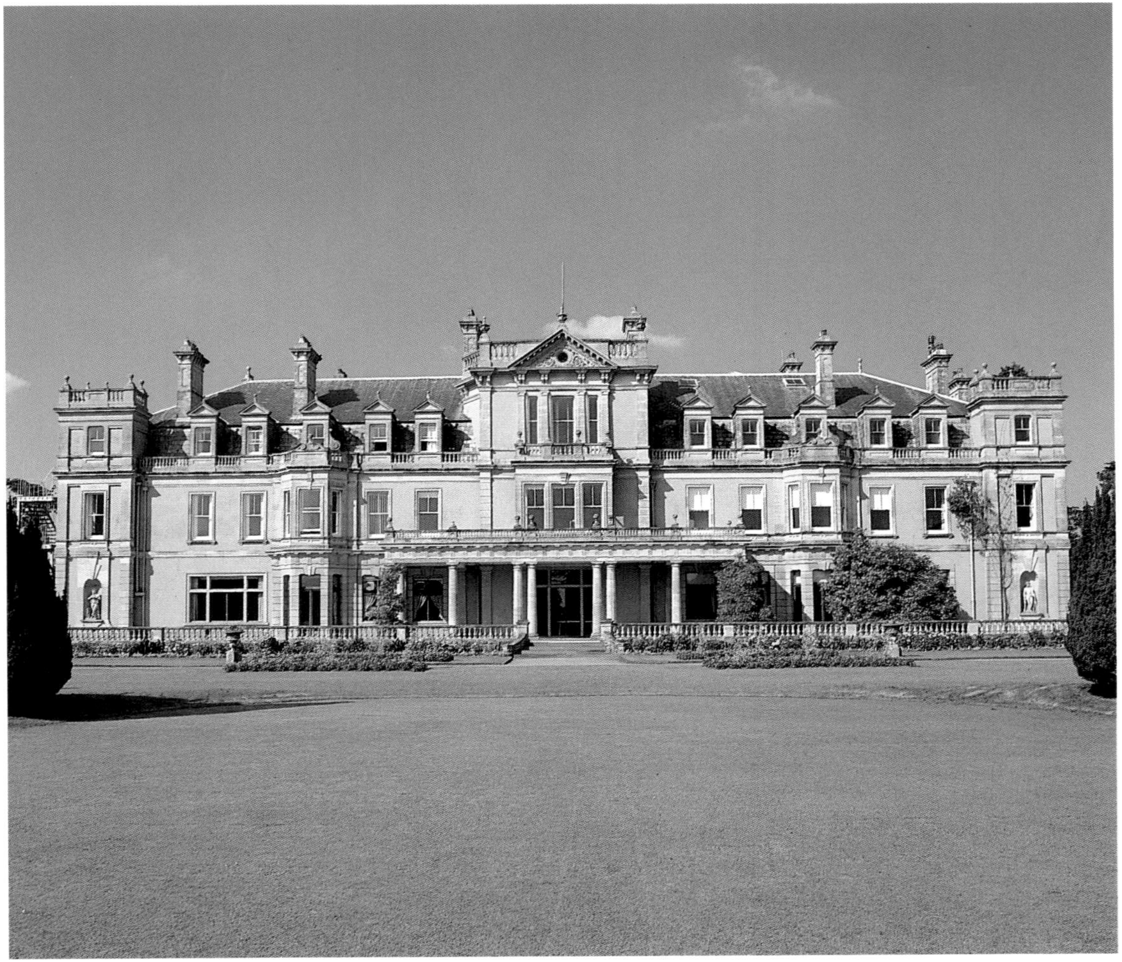

Tri thrigfa bywyd - pen, cwll ac orffed
The three seats of life - the head, the stomach and the lap

Tri peth ni wna les nes curo ei ben - cŷn, polyn tid a thaeog
Three things that do no good unless hit on the head - a chisel, a tethering post and a boor

Tri dyn ni charant eu gwlad - a garo ei fol, a garo gyfoeth, a garo esmwythder
Three men who do not love their country - he who loves his stomach, he who loves wealth and he who loves luxury

Tri glwth byd - môr, dinas ac arglwydd
Three gluttons of the world - the sea, the city and the lord

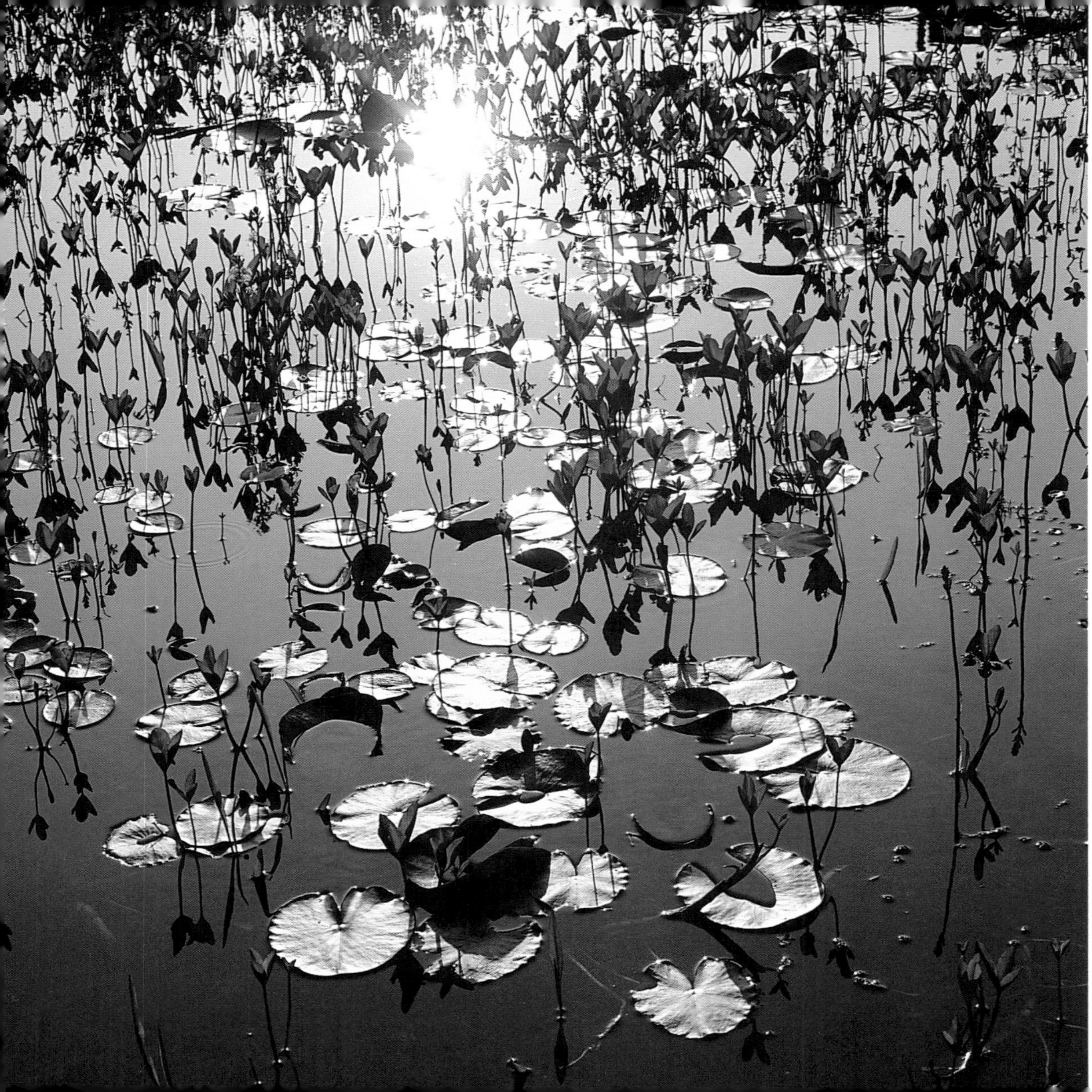

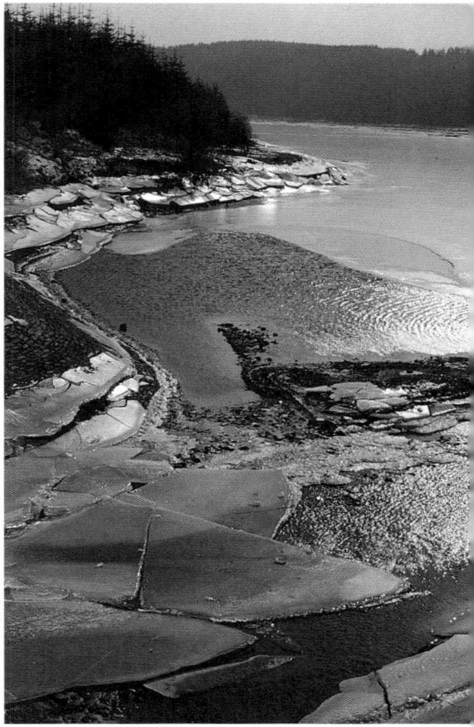

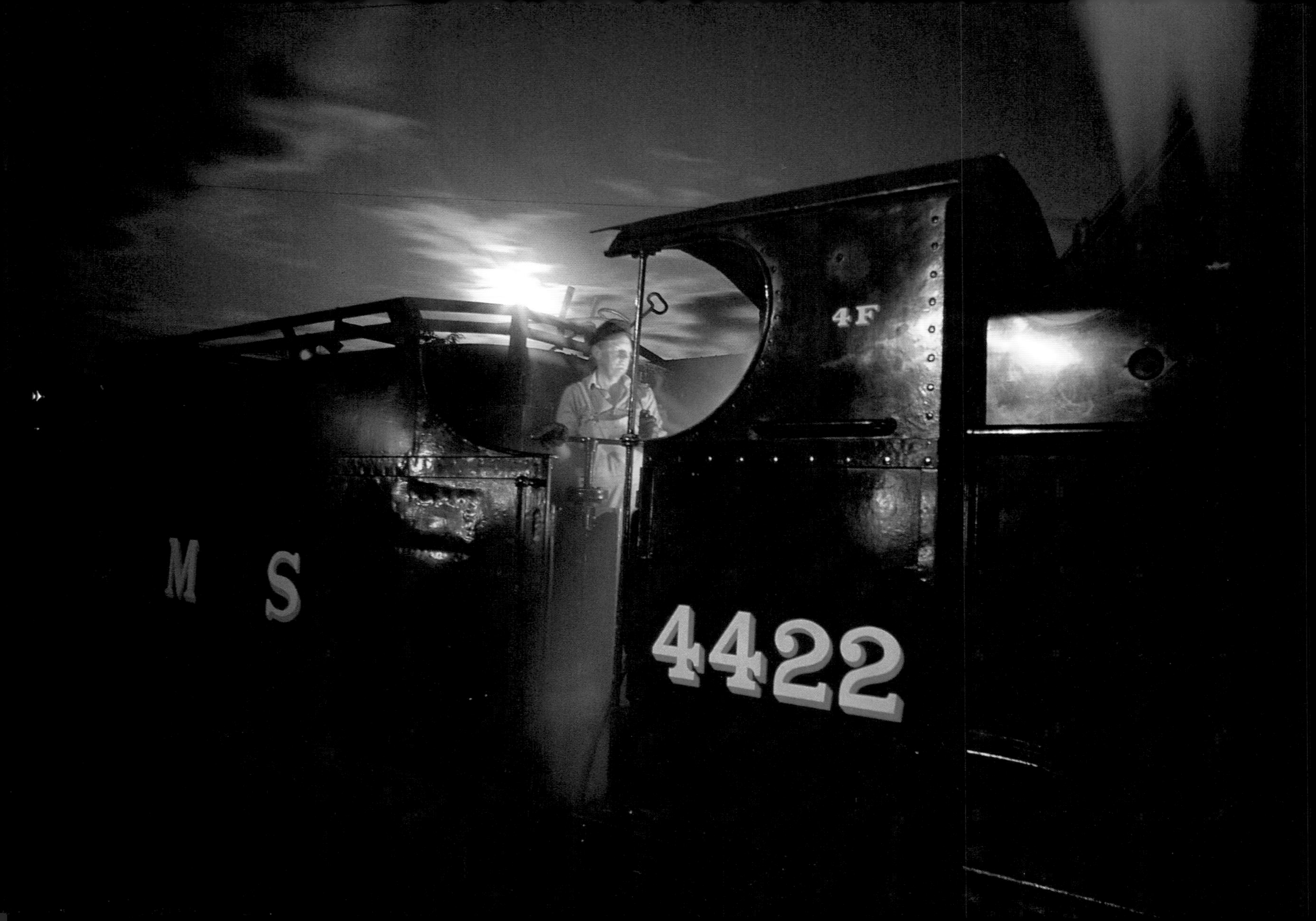
4F
M S
4422

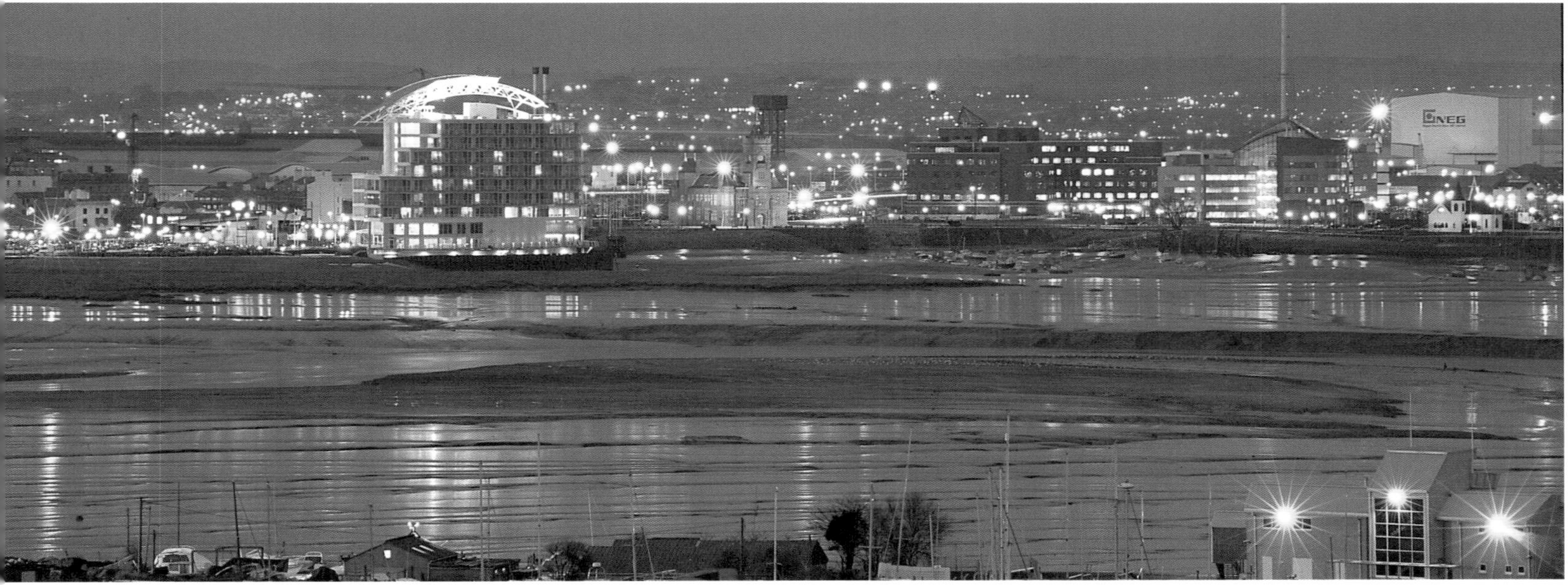

Tri anhebgor iaith - purdeb, amledd a hyweddiant
Three necessities of language - purity, abundance and flexibility

Tri brodyr doethineb - a wrendy, a edrych, a daw
Three brothers of wisdom - he who listens, he who looks and he who is silent

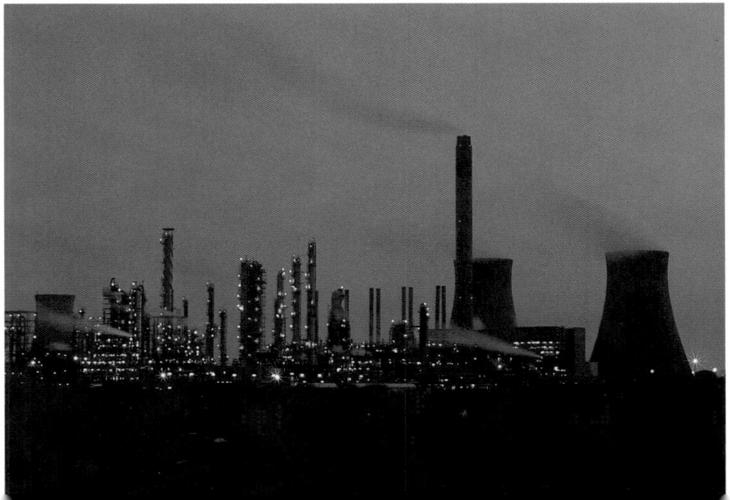

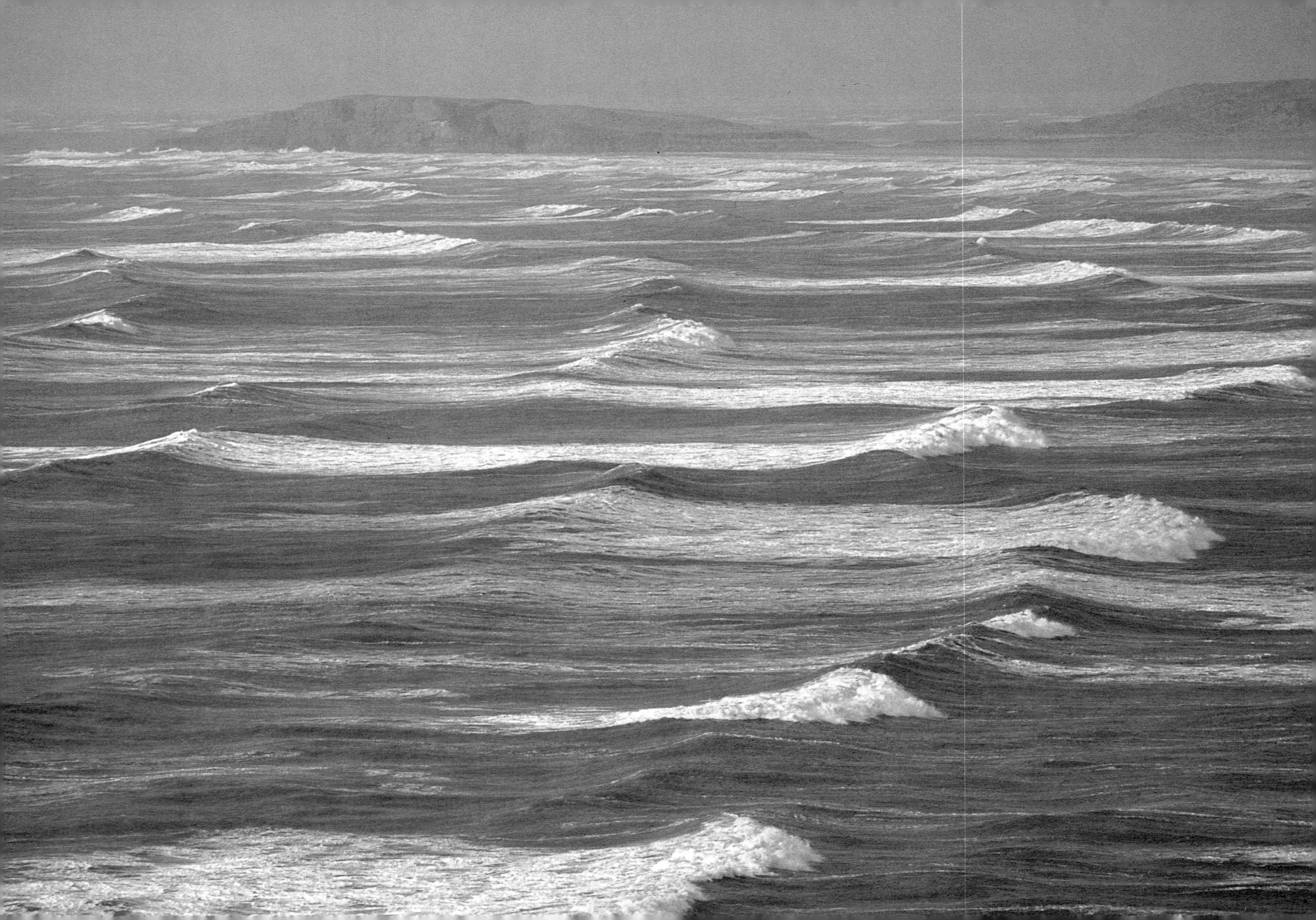

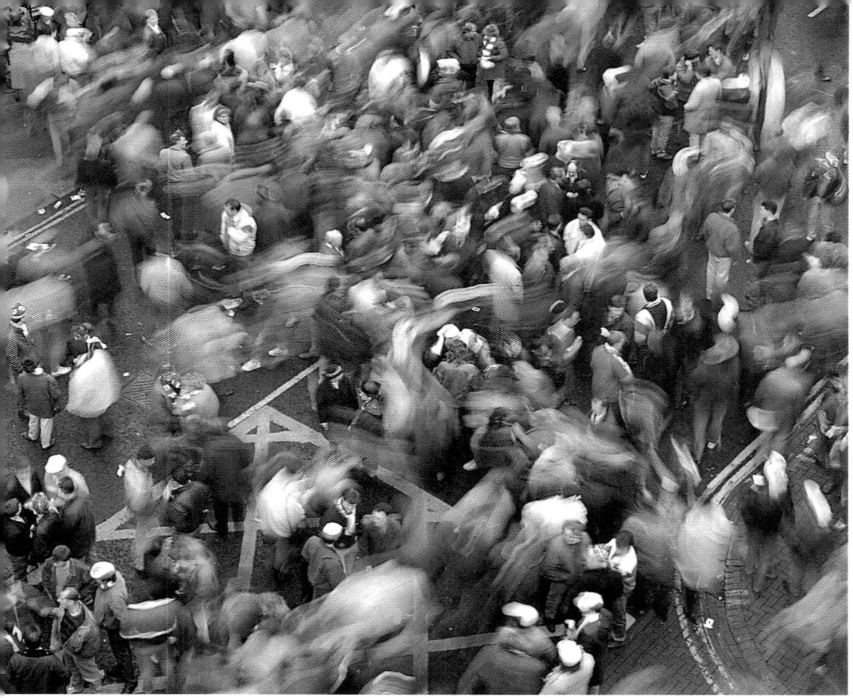

Tair swydd iaith - adrodd, cynhyrfu a dyfalu
Three functions of language - to relate, excite and describe

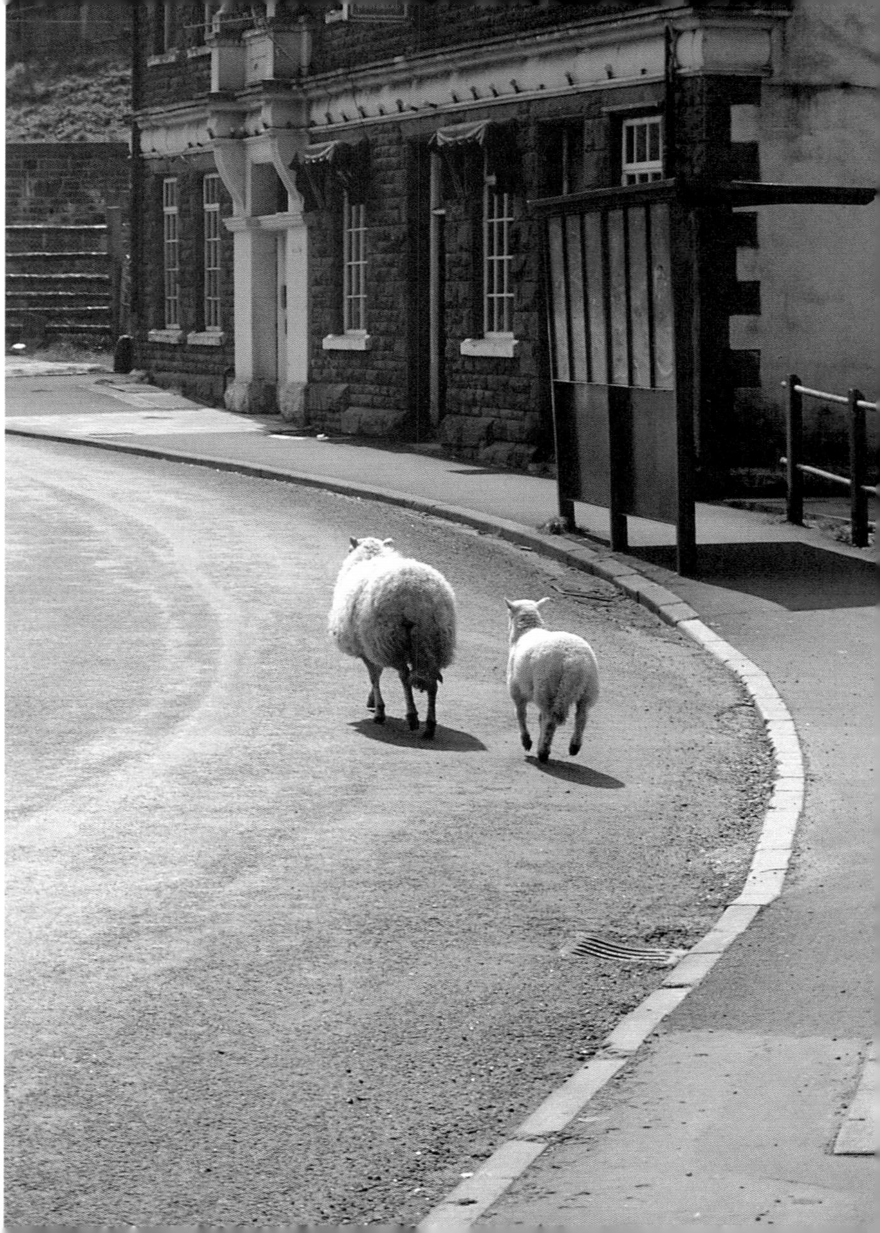

INDEX OF PHOTOGRAPHS

DRINK AND THE TAVERN

TIME, YOUTH AND OLD AGE

HEALTH

THE MILL

FOOD

ENTERTAINMENT

WORK AND CRAFT

THE MISER

THE FOOL

TRAVEL

COMMUNICATIONS

ARISTOCRACY AND THE WEALTHY

KING ARTHUR

TRIADS